D1373997

The
BATHROOM
SPORTS PAGES

———— • ————

Jack Kreismer

RED-LETTER PRESS, INC.
Saddle River, New Jersey

EDITORIAL:
Jeff Kreismer & Kobus Reyneke

TYPOGRAPHY:
Christina Chybinski & Matt Taets

COVER:
Cliff Behum

•

THE BATHROOM SPORTS PAGES
Revised and Updated 2009
Copyright © 2008 Red-Letter Press, Inc.
ISBN-10: 1-60387-101-2
ISBN-13: 978-1-60387-101-3
All rights reserved.
Printed in the United States of America.

Red-Letter Press, Inc.
P.O. Box 393
Saddle River, NJ 07458
www.Red-LetterPress.com

CONTENTS

The
BATHROOM
SPORTS PAGES

———— • ————

HARDBALL TRIVIA

"Baseball, it is said, is only a game. True.
And the Grand Canyon is only a hole in Arizona."

—George F. Will

Candlestick Park, former home of the San Francisco Giants, was the site of the last performance of The Beatles, on August 29, 1966.

•

U.S. Senator Jim Bunning was the first pitcher to win 100 games in each league in the 20th century. Bunning pitched for the Tigers and Phillies in his major league career. While with Philadelphia, Bunning pitched a perfect game on Father's Day in 1964. A father himself, Bunning could field a baseball team. He has nine children.

•

Carl Yastrzemski's average of .3005 in 1968 was the lowest ever to win the AL batting title.

•

Sandy Koufax attended the University of Cincinnati on a basketball scholarship, playing freshman hoops (and baseball) under legendary basketball coach Ed Jucker.

•

Lou Gehrig's salary in 1927, as a member of the Yankees "Murderer's Row," was $8,000.

"Statistics are used by baseball fans in much the
same way that a drunk leans against a street lamp;
it's there more for support than enlightenment."

—Vin Scully

While Joe Tinker, Johnny Evers and Frank Chance are all members of the Baseball Hall of Fame, the tandem was a bit over hyped. At the height of their popularity, they turned just 56 double plays in 4 years. Johnny Evers even led the league once in errors with 44 at second base.

•

The New York Knickerbockers became the first pro baseball club to wear hats - straw hats - in 1852.

•

In 1965, Bert Campaneris of the A's played an inning at each defensive position, a major league first. Three years later, Cesar Tovar of the Twins became the second man to play all the positions in one game. The first man to face him when he took the mound...Bert Campaneris.

•

Former president Ronald Reagan once worked as a radio announcer for the Chicago Cubs in the 1930s. His success gave him the opportunity to pursue acting, where he once played Grover Cleveland, a pitching prospect, in *The Winning Team.*

•

In 1908, Hall of Fame pitcher Walter Johnson pitched three shutouts in four days, allowing a grand total of twelve hits.

> *"I occasionally get birthday cards from fans. But it's often the same message: They hope it's my last."*
> —Former National League Umpire Al Forman

Hall of Fame pitcher Christy Mathewson was an accomplished checkers player. In fact, he once defeated the world checkers champion, Newell Banks.

•

Cesar Geronimo was the 3,000th strikeout victim of both Nolan Ryan and Bob Gibson.

•

Bob Gibson is the last National League pitcher to win the Most Valuable Player Award (1968).

•

On June 15, 1938, Cincinnati's Johnny Vander Meer became the only pitcher in baseball history to throw two consecutive no-hitters. Vander Meer shut out the Dodgers, 6-0, four days after his 3-0 masterpiece against the Boston Braves. Vander Meer's nickname was "Dutch Master," but he also became known as "Double No-Hit" after his historic accomplishment.

•

Charles Dillon Stengel got the nickname "Casey" from his birthplace, Kansas City ("KC"), Missouri.

•

The All-Star Game was dreamed up by *Chicago Tribune* sports editor Arch Ward.

"Never answer an anonymous letter."

—Yogi Berra

In 1952, Bristol, Virginia, pitcher Ron Necciai struck out 27 batters in a nine inning Appalachian League game against Welch, West Virginia.

•

Joe DiMaggio's brother Dom hit in 34 straight games as a member of the Boston Red Sox in 1949. The team that stopped his streak - the New York Yankees.

•

During the 1995 World Series, NBC's Hannah Storm became the first female sportscaster to host a Fall Classic game and ABC's Lesley Visser became the first female sideline reporter, as coverage of the Series was split between two different networks for the first time.

•

Eddie Mathews is the only man to play with the same team (Braves) in three different cities. He began his career in 1952, the Braves final year in Boston. He then played the club's entire 1953 to '65 stay in Milwaukee before playing one year, 1966, in Atlanta.

•

One of the worst home run hitters of all-time was Tommy Thevenow, who in 4,164 career at-bats, hit two homers. Both of Thevenow's home runs came in 1926 with the Cardinals, and both were inside-the-park.

> *"Why does everyone stand up and sing*
> *'Take Me Out to the Ballgame' when they're already there?"*
>
> —Larry Anderson

Officially opened in 1939, the Baseball Hall of Fame is the first such institution devoted to a sport.

•

In 1905, Honus Wagner became the first player to have his autograph branded into a Louisville Slugger baseball bat.

•

The uniform number of baseball comedian Max Patkin was? (That was a statement.)

•

Fenway Park's Green Monster is 37 feet high.

•

In the 2008 Home Run Derby at Yankee Stadium, Josh Hamilton hit a contest record 28 homers in the first round. Hamilton, however, would run out of steam in the finals, losing the title to Justin Morneau despite having 13 more total home runs (35 to 22).

•

On September 27, 1963, the Houston Colt .45s started the first and only all rookie lineup in MLB history against the Mets. Despite future stars like Joe Morgan and Rusty Staub, the freshman team, with an average age of 19 years old, lost to New York, 10-3. Houston's right fielder that day was a little-known player named Aaron Pointer. His better-known sisters had a few hits of their own – performing as the Pointer Sisters.

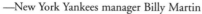

THOUGHTS OF THE THRONE

"It seems to me the official (baseball) rule book should be called the funny pages. It obviously doesn't mean anything. The rule book is only good for when you go deer hunting and run out of toilet paper."

—New York Yankees manager Billy Martin

The 1965 Dodgers featured the big league's first all-switch hitting infield: Wes Parker played first base, Jim Lefebvre was at second, Maury Wills at short, and Jim Gilliam at third.

•

A baseball that landed in fair territory and bounced into the stands was counted as a home run until 1931, when the Baseball Rules Committee decided it should be a ground-rule double instead.

•

Baseball is the only major American sport in which the championship trophy is not named after someone. Technically, it is known as the Commissioner's Trophy.

•

When Cubs manager Whitey Lockman was ejected from a 1973 game, coach Ernie Banks filled in for the last couple of innings of a 3-2 win over the Padres. Thus, Mr. Cub was technically baseball's first African American manager, pre-dating Frank Robinson by nearly two years.

•

Yankee manager Bill Virdon, who piloted New York in 1974 and '75, never won a game in Yankee Stadium. During Virdon's tenure, the Bronx Bombers played their home games at Shea Stadium in Queens while the "House that Ruth Built" underwent renovations.

> *"Baseball is the only orderly thing in a very disorderly world. If you get three strkes, even the best lawyer in the world can't get you off."*
>
> —Bill Veeck

Bob Watson scored Major League Baseball's one-millionth run in 1975.

•

The Houston Astros are the only team to have had Nolan Ryan, Roger Clemens, and Randy Johnson - the top three on the all-time strikeout list - on their roster at one time or another.

•

Rather than retiring a number to honor a player, the Blue Jays have instituted a "Level of Excellence" in the right and left-field areas at the Rogers Centre, where the likes of Joe Carter, Tony Fernandez and Dave Stieb are recognized.

•

Roger Clemens and his wife, Debbie, have four sons: Koby, Kory, Kacy, and Kody (Ks as in strikeouts).

•

In 1951, umpire Frank Dascoli ejected the entire Dodgers' bench after a protest over a controversial call at home. Among those thrown out was Bill Sharman, who became the first major leaguer ejected without ever playing in a single game. That's the same Bill Sharman who had a Hall of Fame career with the NBA's Boston Celtics.

•

The score of a forfeited softball game is 7-0.

> *"Baseball players are smarter than football players.*
> *How many times do you see a baseball team*
> *penalized for too many men on the field?"*
>
> —Jim Bouton

Pitcher Bill Singer is credited with baseball's first save. The statistic made its debut in 1969 when Singer was playing with the Dodgers, and history was made in a 3-2 Los Angeles win over the Reds.

•

When Cardinals' pitcher Jason Marquis and Red Sox catcher Jason Varitek squared off against each other in the 2004 World Series, it was the first time in major league history that Little League World Series participants faced each other as pitcher and batter in the Fall Classic.

•

Former pitcher Tommy John had a doorbell which played *Take Me Out to the Ball Game.*

•

Early in his broadcasting career, Harry Caray would sing *Take Me Out to the Ball Game* to himself. Then, in 1976, White Sox owner Bill Veeck secretly placed a public address microphone in the broadcast booth so the entire stadium could hear Caray. When Caray joined the Cubs' broadcast team in 1982, he took the tradition with him.

•

Satchel Paige earned his nickname from his job as a redcap at a train station where he carried people's "satchels."

> *"The secret of managing is to keep the guys who hate you away from the guys who are undecided."*
> —Casey Stengel

Paul and Lloyd Waner, who played in the outfield together for the Pittsburgh Pirates in the 1920s and '30s, are the only two brothers enshrined in the Baseball Hall of Fame.

•

Long before he got into big trouble for tax evasion, Pete Rose got into a little trouble for parking illegally outside Cincinnati's Riverfront Stadium. The street name on the ticket? Pete Rose Way.

•

Shoeless Joe Jackson got his nickname when he played without his cleats in a minor league game. Suffering from a blister from one of his new spikes, he played in his stockings. When he reached base, a heckler called him a "shoeless son-of-a-bitch."

•

Vida Blue is the last switch hitter to win the American League MVP award, in 1971. Obviously, it wasn't for his .118 batting average, but rather for his 24-8 record, 1.82 ERA and 301 strikeouts that year.

•

The Honus Wagner tobacco card is known as the "Mona Lisa of Baseball Cards" due to its rarity and legend. Wagner objected that his name be used in association with smoking. The American Tobacco Company stopped production of his card, but approximately 50 were still released.

> *"If you don't know where you're going,*
> *you could wind up someplace else."*
>
> —Yogi Berra

When National League umpire Tom Gorman died in 1986, he was buried in his blue umpire's suit, and with a ball and strike indicator in his hand. The count on it was 3-2.

•

A 1985 issue of *Sports Illustrated* contained a fictitious article about Mets pitching prospect Sidd Finch, who threw a 168-mph fastball. In this April Fools article, author George Plimpton tricked readers by making up quotes from real Mets players and staging several photos.

•

Wade Boggs claimed to have eaten a chicken meal before every game he played. Fittingly, his book of chicken recipes is called *Fowl Tips*.

•

Harry "Slug" Heilman was an odd hitter. The Detroit Tigers slugger won the American League batting title every other year from 1921-27.

•

In 1979, Ken Forsch of the Houston Astros hurled a 6-0 no-hitter against the Atlanta Braves. Ken's brother, Bob, pitched a no-hitter in 1978, making them the first siblings to do so. Bob Forsch pitched another no-no for St. Louis in 1983, blanking Montreal, 3-0.

THOUGHTS OF THE THRONE

"I flush the john between innings to keep my wrists strong."

—Former designated hitter John Lowenstein,
on how he stayed ready while on the bench

Pitcher Joe Niekro hit only one home run in his big league career. It came off his brother, Phil.

•

Hank Aaron and Babe Ruth were both members of the Braves when they hit home run number 714.

•

On April 19, 1981, the Rochester Red Wings and Pawtucket Red Sox of the International League were tied at two when play was suspended after 32 innings. The game resumed when the two teams met again later that season and ended after 18 minutes. Pawtucket scored a run in the bottom of the 33rd to win. Among the professional baseball records that still stand from that game are innings, time (8 hours, 25 minutes), strikeouts (60), at-bats (219), and pitches (882). The game featured 25 future big leaguers, including Wade Boggs and Cal Ripken Jr.

•

Eric Davis was known as "Eric the Red" when he played for the Reds.

•

Softball was originally called kitten ball. The game, modified from baseball in 1887 by George Hancock, didn't shed this catty name until 1926.

"Therapy can be a good thing; it can be therapeutic."
—Alex Rodriguez, on the benefits of seeing a therapist

Despite winning 324 games and striking out 5,714 batters, Nolan Ryan never won the Cy Young Award.

•

The 1944 World Series was played by teams from the same city and the same park. The St. Louis Browns faced the St. Louis Cardinals at their mutual home, Sportsman's Park. The Series was won by the Cardinals, four games to two.

•

Al Oliver was the first big league player to wear the number 0. The Rangers outfielder, however, insisted it was an "O" for Oliver, not a zero.

•

During World War II, American GI's reported that Japanese soldiers would shout at them, "To hell with Babe Ruth!"

•

Charlie Brown's favorite baseball player in the *Peanuts* comic strip is Joe Shlabotnik.

•

In 1998, David Wells pitched a perfect game for the Yankees in a 4-0 win over the Minnesota Twins. Coincidentally, Wells went to the same high school as Don Larsen, who pitched a perfect game for New York in the 1956 World Series.

> *"Say this for big league baseball – it is beyond any question the greatest conversation piece ever invented."*
> —Bruce Catton

In 2003, 72- year-old Jack McKeon became the oldest manager to win a World Series when his Florida Marlins defeated the New York Yankees in six games.

•

Before 1859, baseball umpires sat comfortably behind home plate in padded rocking chairs.

•

Triple Play: New York Yankees outfielder Gene Woodling homered off Early Wynn of the Cleveland Indians on June 24, July 24 and August 24, 1951.

•

The symbol "K," used to signify a strikeout, comes from the last letter of the word "struck."

•

In 1885, Art Irwin became the first infielder to wear a glove. He developed the first known fielder's mitt after padding a buckskin glove to protect his two broken fingers. Irwin patented the idea once it caught on.

•

Frank Zupo and George Zuverink formed the only "Z" battery in major league history. The Z-boys twice formed a one-inning battery for the Baltimore Orioles in 1957.

THOUGHTS OF THE THRONE

*"There was no pressure in my at bats.
Everybody was in the bathroom."*

—Hideki Matsui, Yankee outfielder, after hitting two homers in a game while batting behind Alex Rodriguez, who was in quest of his 500th

BASEBALL ‑ 20 QUESTIONS

1. Who was the first Little Leaguer to become President of the United States?

2. The 1962 expansion New York Mets had two pitchers with the same first and last names. Who were they?

3. Phillies great Mike Schmidt was voted starting NL third baseman for the 1989 All-Star Game but didn't play. Why?

4. Who's the only big leaguer to have worn his birthday on his back?

5. What's the greatest amount of pitches a batter can face, without ever lifting the bat off his shoulder, until he either strikes out or walks?

6. A baseball first occurred in 1960 when Detroit traded Jimmie Dykes to Cleveland for Joe Gordon. What was unique about it?

7. Of the top five career home run leaders whose last names begin with "T", two have the exact same name. Do you know it?

8. George "Duffy" Lewis was to Babe Ruth what Mike Lum was to Hank Aaron and what Carroll Hardy was to Ted Williams. What?

9. In 1962, the Cleveland Indians traded Harry Chiti to the New York Mets for a player to be named later. Who became that player?

10. What's the score of a forfeited game?

11. Ted Danson played what fictional retired pitcher for the Boston Red Sox in the hit television series *Cheers?*

12. On August 16, 1954, *Sports Illustrated* made its debut. What baseball player was featured on the first cover?

13. What player with over 3,000 hits had exactly the same amount of hits at home as on the road?

14. What team had the same nine batters go to the plate in an entire World Series?

15. How wide is home plate?

16. What baseball stadium began the tradition of the "Sausage Race?"

17. True or false? Babe Ruth once led the American League in earned run average as a pitcher.

18. Who is the only person to hit a major league home run and score an NFL touchdown in the same week?

19. Who was the only player to hit four home runs in a game and three triples in another?

20. If a player earns a golden sombrero, what has he done?

ANSWERS

1. George W. Bush – Dubya played catcher as a Little Leaguer in Midland, Texas, from 1955 to 1958.

2. Bob Miller and Bob Miller.

3. He retired before the game.

4. Carlos May – His number was 17 and his last name, which appeared above the number, combined with it to form his birth date.

5. Eleven – He's at the plate with a 3-2 count when a base runner gets caught stealing for the third out. He then comes up the next inning and either walks or strikes out following another 3-2 count.

6. They were managers.

7. Frank Thomas.

8. Their only pinch-hitters.

9. Harry Chiti- the only player to ever be traded for himself.

10. 9-0.

11. Sam Malone.

12. Milwaukee Braves third baseman Ed Mathews.

13. Stan Musial, with 1,815 away and 1,815 at home.

14. The 1976 Cincinnati Reds, the first year the DH rule was in effect, used Dan Driessen as their designated hitter and the same eight position players when they swept the New York Yankees.

15. Seventeen inches.

16. County Stadium in Milwaukee – The tradition continued when the Brewers moved into Miller Park in 2001.

17. True – Ruth won the title with an ERA of 1.75 in 1916.

18. Deion Sanders, in 1989 with the Yankees and the Falcons.

19. Willie Mays.

20. He struck out four times.

RIMSHOTS

"Basketball embodies everything our culture now craves: excitement, speed, dynamic personalities, up-close relationships with stars, the exciting physical nature of the contest, and, of course, the incredible suspense that is possible with each game."

—Bill Walton

In 2003, Yao Ming sued Coca-Cola for using his image without permission on Coke bottles that sold in China. The Rockets star, who had just signed an international deal with Pepsi, demanded twelve cents in damages and an apology. The soft drink giant eventually backed down, paid up and said it was sorry.

•

Pete Maravich was forced to retire in 1980 after just ten seasons in the pros due to a leg injury. Because his career was so short, in 1987 Maravich became the youngest player to be inducted into the Basketball Hall of Fame at 39 years of age.

•

Until 1937, after a team scored a basket, rather than simply awarding the other team possession, a jump ball was held at center court. Because the clock continued to run during the stoppage, the actual playing time of the game was significantly reduced.

"Because there are no fours."

—NBA long-range gunner Antoine Walker, when asked why he shoots so many threes

In 2006, Kobe Bryant scored 81 points in a Lakers' win over the Raptors, becoming just the second player in NBA history (after Wilt Chamberlain) to drop 80 in a game. Kobe's worst scoring performance of that entire season was 11 points. The Lakers' opponent that night? Also the Toronto Raptors.

•

The first, and only, pair of teammates to be named co-MVP's of an All-Star Game were Utah's John Stockton and Karl Malone. The two led the West to a 135-132 overtime victory at the 1993 All-Star Game, held fittingly in Salt Lake City.

•

The first dunk contest in 1976 was a creation of the old American Basketball Association. The rules back then made each player attempt certain mandatory dunks, including one ten feet from the basket. Julius Erving took it a step further when he launched himself from the 15-foot foul line to win the contest.

•

The NBA regular season is 82 games, but in 1992, Thurl Bailey played in 84. He began the season with the Jazz, where he played in 13 games. After being traded to Minnesota, who had played fewer scheduled games than Utah at that point, he was able to participate in 71 more.

"I've had to overcome a lot of diversity."
—Drew Gooden

The first five-player men's intercollegiate basketball game was played in January of 1896 in Iowa City. It didn't quite match the excitement of today's game, as the University of Chicago defeated the University of Iowa, 15-12, before a crowd of about 400 people.

•

In 1999, the Chicago Bulls set an NBA record for the fewest points scored in a single game since the introduction of the shot clock in 1954. They failed to break the half-century mark, losing, 82-49, to the Miami Heat.

•

When the fans voted Kobe Bryant to the Western Conference team for the first time in 1998, he became the youngest starter in the history of the All-Star Game, at 19 years and 169 days old.

•

On March 3, 1951, the Temple Owls' Bill Mlkvy, known as "The Owl Without a Vowel," outscored the entire Wilkes College team in a 99-69 win. Mlkvy erupted for 73 points in the game, shooting 32 for 69 from the floor.

•

In his 13-year NBA career, Bill Russell never scored more than 50 points in a game. In fact, his career low in *rebounds* per game, 18.6 in 1968, is just below his career high in *points* per game, 18.9 in 1962.

> *"My career was sputtering until (I) did a 360*
> *and got headed in the right direction."*
>
> —Tracy McGrady

If it's a matter of seconds, Karl Malone comes in first. He finished runner-up in the NBA scoring race a record five times in his career, all thanks to Michael Jordan. The Mailman finished behind M.J. four straight times from 1989-92, and again in 1997.

•

Julius Erving was the first basketball player to endorse an athletic shoe. His Pro Leather Converse sneaker, which would become known simply as "The Dr. J," was released in 1976. The shoe's motto: "Limousines for the Feet."

•

Wendell Ladner is the only non-NBA player to have his number retired by an NBA team. Ladner played just two years with the New Jersey Nets in the ABA, and was admired for his personality rather than his basketball talent. His number 4 was retired by the Nets shortly after he died in a plane crash in 1975.

•

Hall of Famer Bill Russell was the second player chosen in the 1956 NBA Draft. The Rochester Royals, armed with the first pick, gazed into their crystal ball, passed on Russell, and chose Si Green of Duquesne instead.

•

The NBA's foul lane is 12 feet wide.

THOUGHTS OF THE THRONE

"I'm like toilet paper, toothpaste and certain amenities...
I'm proven to be good."

—Shaquille O'Neal, when asked about his
continued effectiveness over the years

In 1969, the ABA's Houston Mavericks set an attendance low for a professional basketball game when 89 people showed up at the Sam Houston Coliseum to see the Mavs in their final home game of the year. Houston had drawn an average of 355 fans per game the previous two months.

•

Before coaching at Georgetown, John Thompson played two years in the NBA for the Boston Celtics from 1964 to 1966. A center, Thompson backed up Bill Russell, earning the nickname "The Caddy" for his role on the team.

•

The first black man to be drafted by an NBA team was Duquesne University's Chuck Cooper, who was selected in the second round of the 1950 draft by the Boston Celtics. Cooper would average just under seven points per game in his six-year career.

•

With Los Angeles leading the Celtics in Game 7 of the 1984 NBA Finals in Boston, die-hard Lakers fan Jack Nicholson began taunting the crowd with the choke sign from his private box. But Nicholson soon became disgusted when the Lakers dropped the lead, so he, in turn, dropped his pants, mooning the entire crowd. Los Angeles lost.

"If Kobe Bryant had a kidney stone, would he pass it?"

—Jay Leno

The 1936 Olympic U.S. basketball team won the first gold ever in hoops, and earned more than just a medal. Each of the players also received a handshake and a laurel wreath from the inventor of basketball, James Naismith.

•

In 2002, Portland's Qyntel Woods was stopped by police for speeding. When he rolled down the window of his car, police smelled marijuana, searched the vehicle, and found the drug. When they asked Woods for proof of license and insurance, the Trail Blazer had neither, so he produced the next best thing for ID – his basketball card.

•

Reggie Miller was born with a hip deformity that caused severely splayed feet, making it hard for him to walk. For four years as a child, he wore leg braces to correct the problem, and doctors questioned if he would ever walk unassisted.

•

Syracuse coach Jim Boeheim has spent his entire college basketball career (player, assistant coach, and head coach) at the school. He enrolled at Syracuse in 1962 as a student, played on the basketball team as a walk-on until 1966, and in 1969 was hired as a graduate assistant. He's been with the program ever since.

"Shaq has gotten so big his toes look like people.
Ooh, he'll get mad at me for saying that.
I'll just dress like a free throw, and he'll miss me."

—D.L. Hughley

Early in his NBA career, Shaquille O'Neal was constantly late for practice and often a source of frustration for Orlando coach Chuck Daly. One day Shaq made it his business to be on time and appeared on the court wearing his shoes... and his birthday suit.

•

At North Carolina, Dean Smith always started all his seniors on "Senior Day," the last home game of the season. One year, when the team included six seniors, Smith opted to put all of them on the floor for the opening tip and willingly took a technical foul, refusing to leave one out of the starting lineup.

•

Kareem Abdul-Jabbar (the former Lew Alcindor) has appeared twice on *Celebrity Jeopardy!*, winning handily both times. In 1994, he defeated Larry King and Alexandra Paul. Four years later, he beat Martina Navratilova and Reggie Jackson in a special "athletes" edition.

•

A former first-round pick of the Nets in 1994, center Yinka Dare set an NBA mark for futility by playing in 77 games and 770 minutes of action before getting his first career assist in 1997. He ended his four-year career with four assists, and more turnovers (96) than field goals (86).

> *"He's one of the best power forwards of all-time.*
> *I take my hands off to him."*
>
> —Scottie Pippen, on Tim Duncan

The expansion Charlotte Bobcats made a "rookie mistake" in their inaugural ticket sales campaign in 2004. Because of a mix-up in the local telephone book, fans who dialed what they thought was the number to order tickets were, instead, directed to a sex chat line!

•

Only four players in NBA history have scored over 30,000 career points. Kareem Abdul-Jabbar is the all-time leader with 38,387. Karl Malone's 36,928 is second, followed by Michael Jordan's 32,292 and Wilt Chamberlain's 31,419 points.

•

In 2006, Epiphanny Prince of Murry Bergtraum HS in New York scored 113 points in a game against Brandeis HS. Prince broke the girls' national prep record previously held by Cheryl Miller, who dropped in 105 points.

•

The NBA Championship Trophy, created in 1978, was renamed for Larry O'Brien in 1984. Unlike awards such as the Stanley Cup, a new Larry O'Brien Trophy is made every year for the winning team to keep permanently.

•

On February 13, 1954, Furman's Frank Selvy scored 100 points in a 149-95 win against Newberry. The game was the first televised

> *"In my prime I could have handled Michael Jordan.*
> *Of course, he would be only 12 years old."*
>
> —Jerry Sloan, Utah Jazz coach

sporting event in the state of South Carolina. Selvy entertained the viewers by hitting 41 of his 66 shots, including a last-second 40-footer to reach the milestone. Earlier that year, Bevo Francis of Rio Grande set a small-school record by scoring 113 points in a 134-91 win over Hillside. Three weeks before that Francis pumped in 116 points against Ashland, but it went unrecognized in the record book because he did it against a two-year school.

•

In 1982, the Boston Celtics selected Indiana's Landon Turner, who had recently been paralyzed in a car crash, in the tenth round of the NBA Draft. GM Red Auerbach did it as a favor to Hoosiers coach Bobby Knight.

•

Oscar Robertson had a record 181 career triple-doubles. But that's nothing compared to what he did during the 1961-62 season. He *averaged* a triple double for the entire year. His numbers: 30.8 points, 11.4 assists and 12.5 rebounds per game.

•

In 1944, Arkansas was forced to decline an NCAA Tournament bid when two of its players each suffered a broken leg when they were struck by a passing car while trying to change a tire. Utah, the team named to replace the Razorbacks, won the national championship.

"No, I clean giraffe ears."
—NBA great Elvin Hayes, when asked if he played basketball

In 2005, Eric James Torpy was sentenced to 30 years in prison after being convicted of robbery. A fan of Larry Bird, Torpy requested that his prison term be increased to 33 years to match his hero's jersey number. His wish was granted.

•

Coaching great Pat Riley, who played both football and basketball at Kentucky, was drafted as a flanker by the Dallas Cowboys in the 11th round of the 1967 NFL Draft. He would later be taken by the San Diego Rockets in the first round of the NBA Draft.

•

Charles Barkley missed the 1994-95 season opener as a result of a rather bizarre ailment. Sir Charles was at an Eric Clapton concert where the bright stage lights caused Barkley to rub his eyes. He ended up burning the first layer of his corneas because of a chemical reaction from hand lotion he'd been using.

•

In 1958, referee Jim Duffy threw the St. Louis Hawks Clyde Lovellette out of an exhibition game for arguing a call. While Clyde may have been run out of the game, he had Duffy running for cover as he got even later that night, showing up at the ref's motel room with a pair of six-shooters loaded with blanks.

"I probably couldn't play for me. I wouldn't like my attitude."
—John Thompson, former Georgetown coach

Up until 1973, NCAA bylaws stated that incoming freshmen were not allowed to play varsity basketball during their first year in school. The rule was intended to eliminate the pressure to perform and to ease their transition to college life.

•

Standing at the foul line in a game against Denver in 1991, Bulls superstar Michael Jordan was kiddingly asked by Nuggets rookie Dikembe Mutombo if he could make a free throw with his eyes closed. Jordan shut his eyes, swished the shot, turned to Mutombo and said, "Welcome to the NBA."

•

WNBA star Lisa Leslie once scored 101 points in a high school game - in one half! With her team, Inglewood Morningside, ahead 102-24 at halftime, the opponent, South Torrance, refused to play the second half. Leslie was just shy of Cheryl Miller's high school record of 105.

•

In 1974, Larry Bird briefly attended Indiana University. Hailing from the small town of French Lick, the 17-year-old Bird could not get used to the massive IU campus, and left before attending a single basketball practice. He worked as a garbage collector before attending the smaller Indiana State the next fall.

THOUGHTS OF THE THRONE

"In basketball, it took only 20 years to go from the outhouse to the in crowd."

—Bill Russell, on how long it took from being a black player on the Boston Celtics to becoming coach and GM of the Seattle Supersonics

Perhaps the worst team in Olympic basketball history was the 1948 Iraqi squad. Playing in only five games, Iraq's average margin of defeat was 86 points, including two losses by 100 points each to Korea and China.

•

Former Michigan star Chris Webber bought himself a self-deprecating reminder of the infamous timeout he tried to call during the 1993 NCAA Championship Game against North Carolina- vanity plates that read "Timeout."

•

The Boston Celtics famous logo of a winking leprechaun was designed by Zang Auerbach, Red's brother, in the early 1950's. Zang had previously worked as a political cartoonist at the now-defunct *Washington Star.*

•

James Naismith's 13 Original Rules of "Basket Ball" were published in January of 1892 in the Springfield College school newspaper, *The Triangle.* "Basketball" was originally two words until it was changed much later in the game.

•

Hall of Fame pitchers Bob Gibson and Ferguson Jenkins both played for the Harlem Globetrotters.

> *"We all get heavier as we get older because there's a lot more information in our heads."*
>
> —Vlade Divac, explaining why he reported to training camp 15 pounds overweight

In 1968, the ABA's Nets were known as the Americans and played their home games in the Teaneck (N.J.) Armory. The team was forced to forfeit a playoff game that year because a circus had already booked the building for the date in question.

•

Former NBA center Manute Bol, at 7'7", was known to block a few shots in his career. The Sudan-born Bol wasn't introduced to the game of basketball until coming to the U.S. at the age of 18. The first time he tried to dunk the ball, he chipped a tooth on the rim.

•

Chris Steinmetz, "The Father of Wisconsin Basketball," was the first big time scorer in the college game. In the 1904-05 season, the 5'9", 137-pound Steinmetz scored 462 of Wisconsin's 681 total points. More stunning was the fact that he scored 23 more points than all opponents tallied against the Badgers.

•

Penny Ann Early became the nation's first licensed female jockey in 1968, but the boys at Churchill Downs didn't take to her too kindly and boycotted the races she entered. The ABA's Kentucky Colonels saw it as a promotional opportunity and hired her for one night, for one inbound pass, making her the first female professional basketball player.

> *"I don't create controversies. They're there long before I open my mouth. I just bring them to your attention."*
>
> —Charles Barkley

BASKETBALL - 20 QUESTIONS

1. What former Laker is the only man to play in the NBA Finals and coach in the Super Bowl?

2. In 1939, H.V. Porter, an official with the Illinois High School Association, came up with what phrase to commemorate a basketball tournament?

3. Who has been on the cover of *Sports Illustrated* more than any other person?

4. Who is the only NBA Hall of Famer to have his Harlem Globetrotters uniform number retired?

5. True or false? When James Naismith invented basketball he was not a citizen of the United States.

6. How many NBA team nicknames do not end in the letter "s"?

7. Mike Krzyzewski was Army's captain and point guard in his junior and senior year. Who was Coach K's coach?

8. Who's the youngest player in NBA history to play in a regular season game?

9. What former Bull is the only player to be picked in the first round of both the NBA and Major League Baseball Drafts?

10. The Los Angeles Clippers have had the number one pick in the NBA Draft once in each of the last three decades (1988, 1998 and 2009). What three big men did they select?

11. The 1987-88 Washington Bullets (now Wizards) featured both the tallest and shortest players in NBA history at the same time. Can you name them?

12. Who was the President of the United States when basketball was invented in 1891?

13. Name the Heisman Trophy-winning quarterback who was drafted by the Knicks in 1994 and spent most of his 11-year career with New York.

14. How long is a basketball court?

15. Violet Palmer and Dee Kantner share what "first" in NBA history?

16. Known as "The Big E," I played exactly 50,000 minutes in my NBA career. Who am I?

17. What former NBA center starred in the movie *My Giant* with Billy Crystal?

18. What former NBA guard had a son who was the second pick in the 1998 NBA Draft and a brother who pitched a no-hitter in the majors?

19. Do you know the international claim to fame of Henry Biasatti?

20. Who is Shawn Corey Carter and what does he have to do with the New Jersey Nets?

ANSWERS

1. Bud Grant - He was a reserve forward on the 1949-50 NBA champion Minneapolis Lakers, and later coached the Minnesota Vikings to four Super Bowls.

2. March Madness.

3. Michael Jordan.

4. Wilt Chamberlain, #13.

5. True - Naismith was born in Ontario, Canada, and did not become a U.S. citizen until the 1920s.

6. Three - Miami Heat, Orlando Magic, and Utah Jazz.

7. Bobby Knight.

8. The Lakers Andrew Bynum, in 2005, at 18 years & 6 days old.

9. Scott Burrell - He was selected 26th by the Mariners in the 1989 MLB Draft and 20th by the Charlotte Hornets in the 1993 NBA Draft.

10. Danny Manning (1988), Michael Olowokandi (1998) and Blake Griffin (2009).

11. 7'7" Manute Bol and 5'3" Muggsy Bogues.

12. Benjamin Harrison.

13. Florida State's Charlie Ward.

14. 94 feet.

15. They became the league's first female referees in 1997- and Palmer became the first female to officiate an NBA playoff game in 2006.

16. Elvin Hayes.

17. Gheorghe Muresan.

18. Henry Bibby – Son, Mike, was selected by the Vancouver Grizzlies in '98, while brother, Jim, threw a no-hitter for the Texas Rangers in 1973.

19. He was the first Italian, and first foreign-born player, in the NBA. Biasatti played for the Toronto Huskies in 1946.

20. Better known as the famous rapper Jay-Z, he is part owner of the team.

EXTRA POINTS

"Football is an incredible game.
Sometimes it's so incredible, it's unbelievable."

—Tom Landry

When the Nebraska Cornhuskers play their home games at Memorial Stadium, it becomes the state's third largest city.

•

A ticket to the best seat in the house for Super Bowl I cost $12. The price was considered exorbitant at the time and the game did not sell out at the Los Angeles Memorial Coliseum. As a result, the very first Super Bowl was blacked out on television locally in Los Angeles.

•

In a game in 1913, Indiana Hoosier punter Clair Scott was forced to kick into a 50-mile-per-hour wind from his own end zone. The ball got hung up in the gusts and Iowa punt returner Leo Dick ran 25 yards forward to catch the ball in the Indiana end zone for a touchdown.

•

The 1974 Bethel High School, Brandt, Ohio, football team just might be the worst ever. They were shut out in all 10 games: 40-0, 53-0, 92-0, 89-0, 50-0, 56-0, 36-0, 33-0, 46-0, and 49-0. The coach's name: Dennis Reck.

"One loss is good for the soul.
Too many losses are not good for the coach."

—Knute Rockne

The Washington Redskins were the Boston Redskins before moving to D.C. in 1937.

•

In February 1912, new U.S. football rules were put into motion. The playing field was decreased from 110 yards to 100 yards, a touchdown was six points instead of five, four downs were allowed instead of three, and the kick-off was moved from midfield to the 40-yard line.

•

In 1968, NBC cut away from the Raiders-Jets football game with a little more than a minute to play to show the movie *Heidi*. The network's offices were deluged with phone calls from angry fans who missed seeing Oakland score two touchdowns in nine seconds to beat New York, 43-32. The contest became forever known as the "Heidi Game."

•

George Blanda played in four different decades - from 1949 to 1975.

•

Albany Firebird Eddie Brown set a professional football single-game record with nine touchdowns against the Minnesota Fighting Pike in an Arena Football League contest in 1996.

> *"Old placekickers never die, they just go on missing the point."*
> –Hall of Fame Kicker Lou "The Toe" Groza

The first NFL Rookie of the Year was Alan Ameche, who won the award as a Baltimore Colt in 1955.

•

Timekeepers estimate that the action in a 60-minute football game actually amounts to 14 minutes.

•

Minnesota Twins catcher Joe Mauer was a *USA Today* and Gatorade national player of the year as a St. Paul, MN, high school quarterback but turned down a football scholarship to Florida State University to enter the Major League Baseball draft.

•

Herschel Walker was third in the Heisman Trophy voting in his freshman year at Georgia. In his sophomore year he was second. In his junior year, he won it.

•

Aldo Donelli is the only man to coach a professional and collegiate team simultaneously. He managed Duquesne University's team while also coaching the Pittsburgh Steelers in 1941.

•

The Canadian Football League's Toronto Argonauts, founded in 1873, are the oldest continuously existing pro football team in North America today.

"I'd just like to put it behind me."
—Peyton Manning, when asked about the alleged "mooning" of a teammate in front of a female trainer

The Campbell's Soup red and white label was inspired by the colors of the Cornell University football team.

•

Unlike baseball, enshrinees do not go into the Pro Football Hall of Fame as a member of a certain team. Every team an inductee played or worked for is listed equally.

•

William "Pudge" Heffelfinger was the first professional football player. He was paid $500 to play for the Allegheny Athletic Association in 1892.

•

In 2003, New Mexico placekicker Katie Hnida became the first female player to score in a Division I-A game. She kicked two extra points in a 72-8 win over Texas State-San Marcos.

•

The first indoor Super Bowl was played at the Superdome in 1978 when the Dallas Cowboys beat the Denver Broncos, 27-10.

•

In 1987, Chicago Bears fans began calling rival Green Bay diehards "Cheeseheads" in reference to their dairy heartland location. The Green Bay faithful not only adopted the epithet with pride, but also decided to wear it as well in the form of huge yellow foam hats.

> *"I've dated girls who were far better looking than the quality of the girls who should be going out with me."*
>
> —Cris Collinsworth, on some of the perks that came with being an NFL player

The original symbol for the Patriots, a minuteman snapping a football, was changed in 1993 to a silhouette of a Patriot head wearing a red-white-and-blue tricorner hat. New England fans have taken to calling it the "Flying Elvis."

•

Sid Gillman was the only head coach of the Chargers for the entire 10 year life of the American Football League. During those years (1960-69), the team originated the phrase "fearsome foursome" for their defensive line anchored by Earl Faison and Ernie Ladd. The term was later appropriated by other NFL teams.

•

Thomas "Hollywood" Henderson, a former Dallas Cowboy and All-Pro outside linebacker (1977), had some good fortune off the field. In 2000, he won the Texas state lottery and took home $28 million.

•

In 1916, the biggest blowout in football history occurred when Georgia Tech crushed Cumberland College, 222-0. Tech scored 32 touchdowns and gained 1,179 yards in the romp.

•

Before a game against the St. Louis Rams in 1981, Baltimore Colts offensive lineman Robert Pratt pulled his hamstring while running out for the coin toss.

> *"In some way, Jerome [Bettis] has touched every person on this team."*
> —Hines Ward

In his 1967 rookie year, Green Bay's Travis Williams averaged an astounding 41.1 yards per kickoff return, a record that may never be broken. He ran back four of his 18 returns for TDs.

•

James Eggink was one of the Montreal Alouettes top choices in the 1996 CFL Draft. The problem? He died in December 1995.

•

It is believed that Notre Dame star George Gipp died of pneumonia in 1920, which he contracted while giving punting lessons. Irish coaching legend Knute Rockne was voted into the College Football Hall of Fame on December 14th, 1951, at 3:27 A.M., in memory of the time and date of Gipp's death.

•

The school with the most college football championships? Yale, 18. Their last title was in 1927.

•

On December 4, 1977, the Tampa Bay Buccaneers walked the plank to their NFL record 26th consecutive loss, a 10-0 defeat at the hands of the Chicago Bears. In Tampa Bay's first NFL season (1976), they were shut out five times in their 14 games. Buccaneers' quarterback Steve Spurrier threw only seven touchdown passes all season. His longest completion was 38 yards.

"If you see a defensive team with dirt and mud on their backs, they've had a bad day."

—John Madden

Former NFL commissioner Paul Tagliabue is a Georgetown graduate and played basketball for the Hoyas. He ranks in the school's top 20 in career rebounds and top 10 in rebounding average.

•

Late golfer Payne Stewart was once sponsored by the NFL and wore the colors and logos of various teams.

•

Quarterback Otto Graham led the Browns to the league Championship Game in each of his 10 seasons with the team, winning on seven occasions. He also played a year of pro basketball for the Rochester Royals, in the 1945-46 season. That year, the Royals won the National Basketball League title.

•

Et tu, Pittsburgh? The Steelers made Notre Dame halfback William Shakespeare their first pick in the 1936 NFL Draft.

•

Jim Kiick, Jack Sack, Clark Gaines, Marion Rushing, Gary Downs, Sam Holden and Willie Thrower (a QB!) were all pro football players.

•

New Orleans was awarded the Saints NFL franchise on November 1, 1966. Coincidentally, November 1 is known as "All Saints Day."

THOUGHTS OF THE THRONE

"The U.S. Congress can declare war with a simple majority, but we need a three-quarters majority to go to the john."
—Baltimore Ravens owner Art Modell, griping about what it takes to revise NFL rules

Jim Thorpe's two Olympic medals were taken away from him when it was discovered that he'd played two seasons of professional minor league baseball before competing in the Games. His medals were reinstated in 1983, thirty years after his death.

•

Former 49er and Jet defensive back and ten-time Pro Bowler Ronnie Lott was one tough customer. Once, when he broke a finger during a game, he cut off the tip of it and kept on playing.

•

The solid-bronze Heisman Trophy is 14 inches long, 13 1/2" high and 6 1/2" wide, and weighs 25 pounds. It is modeled after a player by the name of Ed Smith, who was a member of the now defunct New York University football team.

•

The Packers are the only non-profit, community owned major league professional sports team in the United States today.

•

In 1924 Red Grange dazzled Illinois football fans, accounting for 402 total yards in a 39-14 win over Michigan. After running back the opening kick 95 yards for a touchdown, he scored on runs of 67, 56, and 44 yards, all in the first quarter. He added a 13-yard score and a 20-yard TD pass later in the game.

> *"I feel like I'm the best, but you're not going to get me to say that."*
>
> —Jerry Rice

"Frenchy" Fuqua, a member of the Super Bowl Steelers of the '70s, was one of the flashiest dressers in the NFL and would occasionally appear in public wearing platform shoes that contained live gold-fish in see-through heels.

•

A ninth-round draft pick, Johnny Unitas was cut in training camp by the Steelers in 1955. He would spend the year playing semi-pro football for the Bloomfield Rams for $6 a game and working at a construction site until he was discovered by the Colts.

•

"Hunchy" Hoernschemeyer (the name alone deserves mention in this book) played for the Detroit Lions from 1950 to 1955. In Hunchy's career, he completed 11 passes. Ten were for touchdowns.

•

The pigskin term "sack" was coined by Hall of Fame defensive end Deacon Jones.

•

The longest play in NFL history which did *not* result in a touch-down occurred on December 10, 1972, when St. Louis Cardinals quarterback Jim Hart had a 98- yard pass completion against the L.A. Rams. The wideout on the receiving end was Bobby Moore-better known today as Ahmad Rashad.

> *"Never tell 'em how many lettermen you've got coming back. Tell 'em how many you lost."*
>
> —Knute Rockne

On a 1973 episode of the TV show *M*A*S*H*, the characters listened to the Army-Navy Game on Armed Forces Radio, which Navy won, 42-36. Had the game really taken place, it would have been the highest-scoring Army-Navy contest ever.

•

In 2003, the *Philadelphia Daily News* wrote an article in celebration of Johnny Unitas' 70th birthday. After realizing Unitas had died the previous year, they ran a correction stating: "Johnny Unitas remains dead and did not celebrate his 70th birthday."

•

Former Cowboys coach Tom Landry served in the U.S. Army Air Force during WorldWar II as a B-17 bomber pilot, flying 30 missions and surviving a crash landing in Belgium.

•

Former Broncos defensive end Lyle Alzado once fought an exhibition boxing match against Muhammad Ali in 1979, losing an eight-round decision.

•

The home team must have 24 footballs available for an NFL game; the league provides an additional 12 balls, separate from the scrimmage play supply, specifically for kicking situations to guard against doctoring prior to their use in the game.

> *"When you get hurt, everything hurts - hands, toes, fingers, everything. I can't even play golf. I sound like I'm making popcorn when I get up in the morning."*
> —Lawrence Taylor, on aging

The Vikings were the first team to appear in four Super Bowls-
and the first team to lose four Super Bowls.

•

Baseball's Roger Maris once held the national high school record
for the most TDs scored on returns in a single game, four.

•

In the 1964 pre-season, then-owner Art Modell put a logo on the
side of the Cleveland Browns helmet. The players disliked it so
much (an interlocking "CB"), they ripped it off and the helmets
have been adorn-free ever since.

•

Florida State and Wichita State combined for a record 27 fumbles
in one game. The game took place while three inches of rain fell
during a Tallahassee downpour in 1969.

•

Ernie "The Cat" Ladd was an All-Pro defensive tackle who played
for San Diego, Houston, and Kansas City in the '60s. He was also
the self-proclaimed "King of Wrestling" as the North American
Heavyweight Wrestling Champion in the 1970s.

•

The University of Florida Gators accidentally published a crocodile
on their media guide cover in 2003.

> "My husband is from England and had never seen a football
> game before. So I could tell him anything I wanted.
> I told him it was over at halftime."
> —Rita Rudner

Offensive tackle Orlando Pace was so dominant at Ohio State that the term "pancake" - referring to when a lineman knocks a defender on his back - was coined for him.

•

The Green Bay Packers and the Dallas Cowboys combined for a grand total of minus 11 passing yards on October 24, 1965. Bart Starr and the Packers had an air "attack" of minus 10 yards yet won the game, 13-3.

•

On December 3, 1950, the Cleveland Browns didn't throw a single pass but still beat the Eagles, 13-7. Ironically, Cleveland's only touchdown came when Warren Lahr intercepted one of Philadelphia's 23 pass attempts and ran it into the end zone.

•

Art Rooney, the long-time owner of the Pittsburgh Steelers, was a big-time horse bettor. In one race alone, at Saratoga, he raked in more than $350,000. He bought the Steelers in 1933 from $2,500 he'd won at the track.

•

By the numbers: 77- The number of punts, combined, by Texas Tech and Centenary College, as they played to a 0-0 tie in a driving rainstorm in 1939.

> *"My only feeling about superstition is that it's unlucky to be behind at the end of the game."*
>
> —Duffy Daugherty

FOOTBALL – 20 QUESTIONS

1. Who has the highest lifetime rushing average among all backs in the NFL with a minimum of 750 running attempts?

2. According to NFL rules, how many minutes long is halftime?

3. True or false? Hall of Fame quarterback Steve Young's great-great-great grandfather was baseball Hall of Fame pitching legend Cy Young.

4. What venue was the first site to host a Super Bowl, a World Series and an NCAA Final Four tournament?

5. Who was the first head coach to defeat all 32 NFL teams?

6. Michigan named this center their most outstanding football player in 1934. Forty years later he became President of the United States. Name him.

7. How wide is a football field?

8. The Cleveland Browns retired the uniform number of Ernie Davis after he died of leukemia without ever having played a single NFL game. What was his number?

9. How did the Green Bay Packers win the NFL Championship twice in 1967?

10. What's the score of a forfeited NFL game?

11. Name the former pro football player who was the 2006 champion of the reality TV show *Dancing with the Stars*.

12. What NFL team drafted Joe Namath?

13. True or false? Former Miami Dolphins wide receiver Mark Duper, a favorite target of Dan Marino, went to court to legally change his name to Mark Super Duper.

14. What U.S. vice-presidential candidate was a quarterback who threw for more pass completions and more yards than anyone in the history of the American Football League?

15. What is the only team name retired by the NFL?

16. I was 28 years old when I won the Heisman Trophy in 2000. Who am I?

17. In 1986, this player was drafted in three different sports. He was the #1 pick of the NFL's Tampa Bay Buccaneers, a fourth-round pick of baseball's Kansas City Royals, and a fifth-round pick of the Continental Basketball Association's Savannah Spirits. Name him.

18. Hall of Famers Alan Page and John Hannah were both born, coincidentally, in what city?

19. Name the only team to make a Super Bowl appearance in the 1970s, '80s, '90s, and in the first decade of the 21st century. *(HINT: It's also the only NFL team that has a logo on just one side of its helmet.)*

20. True or false? While at Notre Dame, Joe Theismann changed the pronunciation of his name from "THEEZ-man" to "THIGHS-man" to rhyme with Heisman - as in the trophy.

ANSWERS

1. None other than Randall Cunningham, with a 6.36 yards per carry average. Jim Brown is second at 5.22.

2. 12.

3. False- Young is actually the great-great-great grandson of Mormon leader Brigham Young.

4. The Hubert H. Humphrey Metrodome in Minneapolis, all in a six-month span from October 1991, to March 1992.

5. Tony Dungy.

6. Gerald Ford.

7. 160 feet.

8. 45.

9. They defeated the Cowboys on January 1, 1967 for the 1966 title and beat Dallas again on December 31, 1967 for the 1967 title.

10. 2-0.

11. Emmitt Smith.

12. The St. Louis Cardinals.

13. True.

14. Jack Kemp.

15. Oilers- After the organization moved from Houston to Tennessee and changed the nickname to the Titans, the league decided to put the former name to bed permanently.

16. Florida State's Chris Weinke, the oldest Heisman winner ever.

17. Bo Jackson.

18. Canton, Ohio, the home of the Pro Football Hall of Fame.

19. The Pittsburgh Steelers.

20. True- But the Heisman winner that year pronounced his name Plunkett.

FORE!PLAY

"Golf satisfies the soul and frustrates the intellect. It is at the same time rewarding and maddening – and it is without doubt the greatest game mankind has ever invented."

—Arnold Palmer

At the 1998 Bay Hill Invitational, John Daly hit a three-wood into the water six times on the par-5 6th. He would up with an 18 on the hole.

•

Lingo of the Links: A "toilet flusher" is a putt that swirls around the rim of the hole.

•

Tee off at the "Fra Mauro Country Club" and you'll literally be hitting moon shots. That's the name of the lunar landing spot where Alan Shepard played golf.

•

In 1457, the Scottish Parliament banned golf. The august body felt the time would be better spent practicing archery for defense against the English.

•

At the 1990 Australian Open, Brett Ogle had his kneecap broken by his ball after it ricocheted off a tree.

"You can make a lot of money playing golf. Just ask my ex-wives."
—Lee Trevino

Raymond Floyd used to hang around with his old baseball buddies on the Chicago Cubs so much that his Cubby friends, Ron Santo and Billy Williams, once gave him a locker at Wrigley Field. Said Floyd, "I'd go to the park every morning, take batting practice with them, and shag balls in the outfield. It was great."

•

A survey by the National Golf Foundation revealed that the typical, not pro, golfer averages a 97 for 18 holes. It is said that only one-third of all golfers regularly break 90.

•

The Walker Cup was donated in 1921, by George Herbert Walker, president of the USGA in 1920 and grandfather of President George Herbert Walker Bush.

•

The first British Open was originally called a "General Golf Tournament for Scotland" and was "open" to only eight invited professionals. It was played at Prestwick in 1860.

•

The Polo Golf Derby, played in Hempstead, Long Island, is for golfers and their carts. Players may only leave their carts while putting. It's all about hitting the ball without slowing down. The fastest time and the fewest strokes wins. Talk about being a good driver!

"Last year was pretty amazing. I could have been studying for finals and midterms (at Stanford), but I got my Masters instead."
—Tiger Woods, at the ESPY Awards

The first men-only golf clubs in the U.S. were nicknamed "Eveless Edens."

•

Hollywood hotshots Michael Douglas and Catherine Zeta-Jones bit the bullet and had protective glass installed in their home in Swansea, Wales. The measure taken was not to shield themselves from bullets, but from golf balls due to errant drives on a nearby course.

•

Heading for the 19th hole? Experts say if you play a round of golf, then drink two cocktails, you've just gained more calories than you burned.

•

In 1986, Wayne Grady was disqualified from both the Phoenix Open and the L.A. Open for hitting someone else's ball.

•

The first British monarch to attend the British Open was King George VI. The King appeared at the 1948 Open.

•

The 19th hole at Royal Troon, Scotland is called the "dirty bar" because players are permitted to drink in their golf attire rather than in jacket and tie.

> *"My family was so poor my sister was made in Japan."*
> —Lee Trevino

In 1977, Al Geiberger sunk an eight-foot putt on the final hole of the second round of the Memphis Classic to become the first golfer to shoot a round of 59. Ironically, the lone videotape of Geiberger's round was destroyed in a fire at the only location that had the filmed record.

•

The last day of The Masters in 1968 was not a happy birthday for Roberto De Vicenzo. His signing of an incorrect scorecard gave the title to Bob Goalby. De Vicenzo may best be remembered for his misfortune rather than the fact that, according to the World Golf Hall of Fame, he won an amazing 230 golf tournaments worldwide.

•

President Grover Cleveland decided against taking up golf in retirement, saying he was too fat.

•

Robert Trent Jones is given credit as the first golf course architect to use water hazards in his course designs.

•

Homero Blancas found himself in the rough, so he ever-so-carefully lined up his shot and then hit the ball. It bounced off a palm tree and landed in the bra of a spectator. Blancas conferred with

"You know the old rule:
He who have fastest cart never have to play bad lie."
—Mickey Mantle

Chi Chi Rodriguez as to what he should do and Rodriguez replied, "I think you should play it."

•

When Owen E. Cummings found himself in four inches of water behind a stone wall, he took a mighty swing and topped the ball, which bounced off the wall and into the cup for an Eagle 3. Great shot. Unfortunately, the club head also hit the wall, flew off and ricocheted back into his face, knocking him cold. Although he won the hole, he was carried off and forfeited the game.

•

Did You Know? Americans spend more than $600 million a year on golf balls alone.

•

Amateur Jim Whelehan of Rochester, NY, was playing an 18-hole round in 1992 when he shot a hole-in-one on the fourth hole of the Heather Glen Golf Links in Myrtle Beach, SC. Thrilled by his feat, he decided to play a second round and later that day, same ball, same hole, same result- he aced it once again.

•

The word "tee" is said to be derived from the Scottish term "teay" which is a small pile of sand. Way back when, golfers would make a teay and place the ball on top of it for driving.

"I wish my name was Tom Kite."
—Ian Baker-Finch, on signing autographs

At Uganda's Jinja Golf Course, you must let elephants play through- they have the right of way.

•

A gopher in Winnipeg, Canada, apparently had a passion for snatching golf balls from a neighboring golf course. The folks there found over 250 balls in the animal's burrow.

•

In 1990, Rob MacGregor bounced a golf ball on the face of his sand wedge 3,699 consecutive times. The old record was held by Mark Mooney with 1,764 bounces.

•

On a hot summer day at the 1986 Anheuser Busch Golf Classic, Bill Kratzert managed to lose three balls during play and had to withdraw from the event because he ran out of them. His caddie, trying to lighten the golf bag, didn't bring any extra ones!

•

"Do you believe in miracles?!" That famous line spoken by Al Michaels to describe the 1980 U.S. Olympic hockey team's win over the Soviet Union is used by the sportscaster to this day. Michaels admits, "It's usually on the golf course after a long birdie putt."

THOUGHTS OF THE THRONE
"The wind was so strong, there were whitecaps in the Porta-John."

—Joyce Kasmierski, at the 1983 Women's Kemper Open

Did You Know? According to the *Guinness Book of World Records*, the longest drive of all time on a regulation course was 515 yards, by Michael Hoke Austin in 1974.

•

There are approximately 32,000 golf courses in the world.

•

In 1993, Germany's Bernhard Langer lodged a ball twenty feet up in a tree while playing in a tournament in England. Langer climbed the tree and knocked the ball out. Afterwards, when asked what club he had used, Langer responded, "A tree iron, of course."

•

In 2006, 12-year-old Blake Hadden from North Augusta, South Carolina, recorded two holes-in-one in the 11-12 age group at the Future Masters. Hadden aced the 83-yard number 5 hole and the 140-yard number 11 hole at the Dothan Country Club in Alabama.

•

Hollywood stars presented the golfers to the gallery when Los Angeles hosted the PGA Championship in 1929. Actress Fay Wray introduced Walter Hagen as "The Opium Champion of Great Britain."

•

On a goodwill tour of South America, Sam Snead was about to hit a bunker shot when an ostrich attacked him. The bird was appar-

> *"I find it to be the hole-in-one."*
>
> —Groucho Marx, on golf's toughest shot

ently interested in Snead's trademark straw hat. When Snead put up his hand to protect his face, the ostrich bit it. Slammin' Sammy was unable to play golf for two weeks.

•

In 1973, Arthur Thompson shot a round of 103 at the Uplands Golf Course in British Columbia. Not bad for a man who was 103 years old.

•

At the 1987 Kemper Open, Greg Norman lost his temper and tried to throw his ball into a water hazard. It became obvious that his golf swing was better than his pitching arm after he hit playing partner Fred Couples in the chest.

•

JoAnn Washam is the only golfer to ace two holes in the same LPGA tournament. Washam did it in the second and final rounds of the 1979 Women's Kemper Open.

•

Grantland Rice suggested that the first Masters, in 1934, be held in late March so baseball writers returning north from spring training could cover the tournament.

> *"Golf and women are a lot alike. You know you are not going to wind up with anything but grief, but you can't resist the impulse."*
>
> —Jackie Gleason

While playing in Sweden in 1990, Steve Elkington was waiting for a ruling when he absentmindedly snapped off a blade of grass to chew on. For that, the officials gave him a two-stroke penalty for touching any impediment in a hazard. By tournament's end, it cost him $5,000.

•

The largest collection of golf books in the world belongs to the USGA Museum and Library, which has a collection of golf magazines dating back to 1880.

•

When rain washed out the first two rounds of the 1983 Hong Kong Open, Greg Norman practiced by driving golf balls out the open window of his hotel room into the harbor. He won the tourney.

•

At the 1998 NEC World Series of Golf, Lee Janzen left a putt so close to the cup he was sure it would go in -and it did, after 20 seconds. The problem was that the rules call for only 10 seconds. Alert TV viewers caught the violation, and tournament officials disqualified Janzen for signing an incorrect scorecard.

•

After a Pro-Am at Doral in 1970, Raymond Floyd wrote his front-side score of 36 in the space reserved for the ninth hole. He signed

"They call it golf because all of the other four-letter words were taken."
—Raymond Floyd

the card and ended up with a round of 110.

•

Sam Snead was playing in a tournament on the day of the 1948 presidential election. As early returns started to come in, someone mentioned to Snead that Dewey was leading. "What'd he go out in?" Snead asked.

•

President George W. Bush and future wife Laura spent their first date at a miniature golf course.

•

The most popular name for a golf course in the U.S. is "Hillcrest."

•

Clayton Heafner was known as a fiery competitor by his fellow pros. Just before he was about to tee off at the 1941 Oakland (CA) Open, the marshal mispronounced his name. Insulted, Heafner withdrew from the tournament.

•

In 1899, golfers at the Atlantic City (N.J.) CC came up with the word "birdie" when George Crump put his second shot inches from the hole on a par-4 after his ball hit a bird in flight.

•

Jack Nicklaus holds the record for the longest time between victo-

"Golf is a dumb game. Hitting the ball is the fun part of it, but the fewer times you hit the ball, the more fun you have. Does this make any sense?"

—Lou Graham

ries at The Masters. Nicklaus first won the tournament in 1963 and then again in 1986, a span of 23 years.

•

Bathroom readers- that means you – take note: Walter Hagen signed autographs as "W.C. Hagen" until he went to England and discovered that "W.C." actually meant "water closet", as in bathroom. From then on, his John Hancock always consisted of his full name.

•

Dave Ragaini used a 3-wood at a 207-yard, par-3 hole at Wykagyl Country Club at New Rochelle, New York and hit a hole-in-one. Oh, yes- he was standing on his knees at the time!

•

In 1965, Robert Mitura shot the ace of all aces with his 440-yard hole-in-one at the 10th hole of the aptly-named Miracle Hills GC in Omaha, Nebraska. Mitura was aided by a 50 mph wind and a 290-yard drop-off.

•

In 1929, James Cash hit a drive from the tee to the edge of the cup on a par-3 hole. As he started down the fairway to putt out, an earth tremor rolled past the course and tipped the ball in for a hole-in-one.

"I've just played World War II golf - out in 39 and back in 45."
—Lee Trevino

Sam Byrd is the only man to play in both a World Series and a Masters Tournament. He played in the 1931 Series for the Yankees and finished in the top five in both the 1941 and 1942 Masters.

•

Gene Littler has the dubious distinction of playing in The Masters the most times without winning it. Littler entered 26 Masters between 1954 and 1980.

•

The injury that caused Lee Janzen to withdraw from the 2003 Wachovia Championships in Charlotte provided some rib-tickling humor for his fellow PGA players – literally. Janzen hurt his ribs playing Ping-Pong.

•

Girl Talk: Over 6 million women in the U.S. play golf, according to the National Golf Foundation; 63 percent of female golfers are 40 or older, said a *Golf Magazine* report; and 2 out of 3 new golfers are women.

•

In 1954, architect Robert Trent Jones received numerous gripes about the par-3 4th hole he had designed for the upcoming U.S. Open at Baltusrol. Jones decided to play it himself and recorded a hole-in-one.

> *"I had a wonderful experience on the golf course today. I had a hole in nothing. Missed the ball and sank the divot."*
>
> —Don Adams

In the 1938 movie *Carefree*, Fred Astaire performed a dance solo in which he hit a row of golf balls while tap-dancing. The solo required almost 1,000 practice shots, 10 days of rehearsal and 2 days of filming. On-screen, the dance lasted 3 minutes.

•

Jack Nicklaus once traded in his golf cart for a helicopter to play eighteen different holes on eighteen different courses in eight hours and forty minutes, raising $590,000 for charity.

•

Did You Know? According to *Golf Digest*, the odds of making two holes-in-one in a round of golf are 67 million to one.

•

The world's first NFL-themed golf course, the Cowboys Golf Club, is located in Grapevine, Texas. A tribute to the Dallas Cowboys, historical illustrations and markers about the team's history are interspersed around the course and in the clubhouse.

•

On June 18, 1987, at the Warrenpoint Golf Club in Down, Ireland, James Carvill played the fastest 18-hole round in history-27 minutes!

THOUGHTS OF THE THRONE

*"I'll get up at five in the morning to do only two things:
go to the bathroom and play golf."*
—Jim McMahon

GOLF - 20 QUESTIONS

1. Name the only sports individual to have been given two New York City ticker-tape parades.

2. What now-famous golf clothing item did the Brooks Uniform Company manufacture in 1937?

3. What LPGA Hall of Famer is married to baseball's 1986 World Series MVP, Ray Night?

4. The USGA recommends that the flagstick be at least how tall?

5. What is a hole-in-one on a par-5 called?

6. True or false? Former First Lady Nancy Reagan is an honorary member of the LPGA Hall of Fame.

7. What movie was filmed at the Rolling Hills Golf Resort in Ft. Lauderdale, Florida?

8. "It is true that my predecessor did not object as I do to pictures of one's golfing skills in action. But neither, on the other hand, did he ever bean a Secret Service agent." Who was John F. Kennedy talking about?

9. Playing by the rules: It's pouring rain and the course is already soaked. Can John Daly play barefoot?

10. In 1986, Jack Nicklaus became the oldest player to win The Masters. How old was he?

11. This mobster accidentally shot himself in the foot with a gun he had hidden in his golf bag at the Burnham Woods Golf Course in 1928. Name him.

12. Finish the following golf-design credo of architect Robert Trent Jones: "Hard par, easy _____."

13. What's the maximum number of clubs a player can carry?

14. What Canadian singer owns Le Mirage golf course, near Montreal?

15. Arnold Palmer hails from the small town of Latrobe, Pennsylvania. It's also the same neighborhood where what legendary children's television show host was born?

16. Can you identify "The" Walrus, Zinger and Hawk?

17. You might say that Jerry Pate, Doug Weaver, Nick Price and Mark Wiebe were holding all the cards on the sixth hole in the 1989 U.S. Open at Rochester's Oak Hill Country Club. Why?

18. Who has appeared on the cover of *Golf Digest* the most times?

19. Who is the only female golfer to shoot a 59 in competition?

20. In 1899, the U.S. Patent Office granted patent 638,920 to African-American George F. Grant for what invention?

ANSWERS

1. Bobby Jones.

2. The Green Jacket- Originally made for all the members of Augusta National, the green jacket became the symbol of The Masters winner in 1949 when Sam Snead became the first to wear it.

3. Nancy Lopez.

4. 7 feet.

5. A condor (triple-eagle and double-albatross are also correct).

6. False – But another former First Lady is- Betty Ford.

7. *Caddyshack.*

8. Dwight Eisenhower.

9. Not according to the USGA.

10. 46.

11. Al Capone.

12. Bogey.

13. 14.

14. Celine Dion.

15. Mr. (Fred) Rogers.

16. Craig Stadler, Paul Azinger and Ben Hogan.

17. All four aced the hole.

18. Jack Nicklaus.

19. Annika Sorenstam.

20. The golf tee.

SPORTS SHORTS

"Sports is the toy department of life."
—Howard Cosell

FIRST THINGS FIRST

In his first NFL game, Walter Payton carried the ball eight times for a total of zero yards.

•

In 1996, the U.S. defeated China, 2-1, to win the first women's soccer gold medal match in Olympic history.

•

In 1911, hometown boy Ray Harroun won the first Indianapolis 500 with a blistering average speed of 74.6 miles per hour.

•

On August 4, 1982, Joel Youngblood became the first major leaguer to get a hit for two different teams in two different cities on the same day. In the afternoon in New York, the Mets infielder-outfielder singled in the winning run against the Cubs and Ferguson Jenkins. He was then traded to Montreal and that evening in Philadelphia, he donned an Expos uniform in time to hit another single off the Phillies Steve Carlton.

"Fear was absolutely necessary.
Without it, I would have been scared to death."
—Floyd Patterson, former heavyweight champ

In 1986, an NBA first, and probably last, occurred when a Suns-Supersonics game was called due to rain. A heavy downpour and a leaky roof on the Seattle Center Coliseum forced officials to stop action in the second quarter. The contest was finished the following day, with Phoenix winning, 114-97.

•

In 1985, Lynette Woodard became the first woman to play for the Harlem Globetrotters. Woodard, who captained the 1984 Olympic gold medal team, scored seven points in her debut. She spent two years with the Globetrotters

•

In 1989, Javier Sotomayor of Cuba became the first person to high jump over eight feet (the equivalent of jumping over the crossbar of a soccer goal).

•

In 1892, Benjamin Harrison became the first president to attend a Major League Baseball game. Cincinnati downed Washington, 7-3, in a National League contest that went 11 innings.

•

Bill Russell, in 1979, became the first basketball personality to host *Saturday Night Live.*

"A couple in Corpus Christi, Texas, named their son 'ESPN' after the sports channel. The parents said the boy is okay with his name, but he's very jealous of his baby brother, 'ESPN2.'"

—Conan O'Brien

Sam Snead was the first golfer to shoot a score lower than his age in a PGA tournament. He shot a 66 at the Quad Cities Open in 1979 at the age of 67.

•

Bob Mathias of the U.S. was the first to win two straight gold medals in the decathlon at the Olympics, in 1948 and 1952.

•

The first woman in modern times to carry the Olympic torch was Norma Enriqueta Basilio Satelo, who lit the flame in Mexico City in 1968.

•

When Dodger Stadium first opened in 1962, it had no drinking fountains.

•

In 1935, President Franklin Delano Roosevelt pressed a button at the White House that turned on the lights for Major League Baseball's first night game. More than 20,000 fans watched at Crosley Field in Cincinnati as the Reds beat the Phillies, 2-1.

•

The Chicago White Sox became the first team in World Series history to win two games on the same calendar date. Game Three of the 2005 Series, which went 14 innings, ended at 1:19 a.m. Central

> *"On the day of the race a lot of people want you to sign something just before you get in the car so that they can say they got your last autograph."*
>
> —A.J. Foyt

Time on Wednesday, October 26. Game Four ended at 11:01 p.m. that night. (Chicago swept the Houston Astros.)

•

Patrick Ewing was the first player ever chosen in the NBA Lottery.

•

Tom Cheney pitched the Washington Senators to a 2-1, 16-inning win over the Baltimore Orioles on September 12, 1962. In doing so, he became the first hurler in big league history to strike out 21 batters.

•

Ernie Davis became the first African-American player to be awarded the Heisman Trophy in 1961.

•

Craig Biggio was the first player to make the All-Star team as a catcher and then a second baseman (in 1991 and '92).

•

At the 2005 Indianapolis 500, Danika Patrick made history by becoming the first woman to ever lead the race. Patrick wound up finishing in fourth place.

•

Albert Pujols became the first in Major League Baseball history to hit 14 home runs in the month of April, in 2006. Alex Rodriguez became the second, in 2007.

"Why doesn't the fattest man in the world become a hockey goalie?"
—Steven Wright

In 2002, Mariners outfielder Mike Cameron became the 13th major leaguer to hit four homers in one game in a 15-4 win over the White Sox. The first two dingers followed homers by second baseman Bret Boone, making it the first time the same two teammates hit back-to-back homers twice in one inning.

•

In 1977, Seattle Slew became the first unbeaten horse to win the Triple Crown.

•

The first Super Bowl which was given a Roman numeral was IV.

•

Keith Jackson, Howard Cosell and Don Meredith were the first announcers on *Monday Night Football.*

•

Bob Griese of the Miami Dolphins was the first NFL quarterback to ever wear glasses in a game. His spectacles are on display in the Pro Football Hall of Fame.

•

In 1967, the Green Bay Packers beat the Kansas City Chiefs, 35-10, in the first game between champions of the NFL and AFL - or Super Bowl I. Players on the winning team in the first Super Bowl received $15,000. The losers got $7,500.

THOUGHTS OF THE THRONE
"I threw the kitchen sink at him.
He went into the bathroom and threw back the tub."
—Andy Roddick, commenting on his loss to Roger
Federer at the 2004 Wimbledon tennis tournament

Roger Bannister, the first person credited with a sub four-minute mile, didn't break this barrier in an official race. Bannister was actually paced by two runners on that record-shattering day in 1954.

•

Olympic gold medal gymnast Mary Lou Retton was the first female to appear on the front of a Wheaties box.

•

In horse racing, the favorite finishes first less than 30 percent of the time.

• • •

SETTING THE RECORD STRAIGHT

In 2001, the Carolina Panthers had the distinct displeasure of becoming the first NFL team to lose 15 straight games in a season.

•

Between his tennis losses to Igor Andreev in April 2005 and Roger Federer in May 2007, Rafael Nadal won 81 clay court matches, the most consecutive victories on a single surface.

"Men forget everything; women remember everything. That's why men need instant replays in sports. They've already forgotten what happened."

—Rita Rudner

When Indiana defeated North Carolina in 1981 for their fourth title, the school became the first to win an NCAA championship in four different decades. Their previous titles were in 1940, 1953, and 1976.

•

Broadcasting legend Chick Hearn called every single Los Angeles Lakers game from the season opener in 1965 to December 2001, a total of 3,338 consecutive contests.

•

Ted St. Martin made a place for himself in Guinness when he sank 2,036 basketball free throws on June 25, 1977 - consecutively.

•

Junior welterweight Julio Cesar Chávez went undefeated for 89 consecutive bouts and retired with a ring record of 108 wins, 6 losses and 2 draws, with 87 knockouts.

•

Joe DiMaggio's 56-game hitting streak included 56 singles and 56 runs scored.

•

In 2004, Lawrence Frank began his NBA New Jersey Nets coaching career with 13 consecutive victories, the longest winning streak ever for a rookie in any of the four major professional sports.

"I want to be the fastest woman in the world...in a manner of speaking."
—Race car driver Shirley Muldowney

In 1925, basketball's longest winning streak came to a halt. It wasn't the Lakers or UCLA, but Passaic (N.J.) High School. Passaic won 159 straight games over five years before being tripped by Hackensack.

• • •

SLAP SHOTS

On March 23, 1952, Chicago's Bill Mosienko scored three goals faster than you could say "hat trick." Mosienko's goals all came within 21 seconds during the third period in a 7-6 win over the Rangers.

•

In the 1970s, the Macon, Georgia, minor league hockey team was called the Macon Whoopies after a song of almost the same name, *Makin' Whoopie.*

•

Before the NHL Draft was implemented, the Montreal Canadiens had first dibs on any French-speaking player.

•

The Boston Bruins purchased the rights to future Hall of Famer

"As a nation we are dedicated to keeping physically fit - and parking as close to the stadium as possible."
—Bill Vaughan, writer

Bobby Orr when he was just 14 years old.

•

Hockey superstar Wayne Gretzky was presented with a Rolls-Royce when he scored his 802nd goal, passing Gordie Howe to become the NHL's all-time leader. The license plate…"GOAL802." The Great One wound up with a career record total of 894 goals.

•

A hockey player is afforded 24 square feet in which to attempt a goal. It's six feet wide and four feet high.

•

The original Stanley Cup was worth $48.67 when Lord Stanley of Preston donated it in 1893.

•

Quick! Who did the U.S. Olympic hockey team beat for the gold in 1980, in Lake Placid, NY? The answer: Finland. Many people think it was the Soviet Union, but that was the contest which enabled the U.S. to advance to the finals against the Finns.

•

In 1981, the Buffalo Sabres entered the NHL record book when they scored nine goals in the second period of a 14-4 win over Toronto. The old record of eight goals in a period had been held by…Toronto.

> *"When I was a kid in Houston, we were so poor we couldn't afford the two letters, so we called ourselves po'."*
>
> —George Foreman

Baseball's 1991 Cy Young Award winner, Tom Glavine, was a 1984 fourth-round pick of the NHL's Los Angeles Kings.

• • •

MOTHERS OF INVENTION

David Mullany invented the Wiffle Ball in 1953.

•

The batting donut was invented by former Yankee catcher Elston Howard.

•

Ken "Hawk" Harrelson, currently a White Sox commentator, was the first to wear a batting glove in a big league game.

•

Golf legend Gene Sarazen introduced the sand wedge in 1932.

•

Author Rudyard Kipling invented the red golf ball for playing in snow.

•

In 1954, the NBA adopted the 24-second shot clock, an invention of Syracuse Nationals owner Danny Biasone. The Syracuse owner

"Anthropologists have discovered a 50-million-year-old human skull with three perfectly preserved teeth intact. They're not sure, but they think it may be the remains of the very first hockey player."

—Jay Leno

came up with 24 seconds by dividing 2,880 (the number of seconds in a game) by 120 (the average number of shots in a game).

•

Racquetball was invented in 1950 by Joe Sobek at the Greenwich, Connecticut, YMCA.

• • •

THE NAME GAME

The NBA's Rockets, who at one time played in San Diego, were originally named for the area's motto, "A City in Motion." When the team moved to Houston, home of the NASA Space Center, the nickname fit even better.

•

On the Vancouver (now Memphis) Grizzlies original franchise application to the NBA, the team name was listed as the Mounties. However, the government of Canada took exception to it, claiming the name was trademarked, and forced the team to change it.

•

Kobe Bryant's unique first name comes from a type of Japanese steak, as "Kobe beef" is produced from cattle in the city of Kobe,

"Take boxing, the simplest, stupidest sport of all. It's almost as if these two guys are just desperate to compete with each other, but they couldn't think of a sport. So they said, "Why don't we just pound each other for forty-five minutes? Maybe someone will come watch that."
—Jerry Seinfeld

Japan. His parents originally saw the name on a menu while eating at a restaurant prior to his birth.

•

The Green Bay Packers were founded in 1919. That name- "Green Bay Packers" -is the oldest team name still in use in the NFL.

•

Tennis great Jimmy Connors was dubbed "le Grognon" by the French - or "the Grunter."

•

Hall of Fame quarterbacks Johnny Unitas and Dan Marino share the same middle name - Constantine.

•

Joe Louis dropped his last name when he began his boxing career. He was born Joseph Louis Barrow.

•

Sportswriter Caswell Adams coined the name "Ivy League."

•

Even longer than the NBA's 7'2" Dikembe Mutombo is his full name: Dikembe Mutombo Mpolondo Mukamba Jean Jacque Wamutombo. The 48 letters are more than twice the size of Mutombo's size 22 shoes.

THOUGHTS OF THE THRONE

"Raise the urinals."

—Darrel Chaney, on how management
could keep the Atlanta Braves on their toes

Connie Mack's real name is Cornelius McGillicuddy.

•

Baseball's Cleveland Indians were originally called the Spiders.

•

Golfer Ben Crenshaw earned the nickname "Tarzan" by hitting so many drives into the woods.

•

"Phillies" is the oldest nickname for a professional sports franchise in America.

•

Former San Antonio Spurs center David Robinson, "The Admiral," was actually a Lieutenant Junior Grade in the Navy.

•

Jack Nicklaus acquired his nickname from his high school, the Upper Arlington (Ohio) Golden Bear.

•

Miniature golf was originally called "Tom Thumb Golf."

•

Legend has it that famed Alabama coach Paul Bryant, as a 14-year-old, was given the nickname "Bear" after he successfully wrestled a muzzled bear for a theater promotion.

*"I put Sugar Ray Robinson on the canvas —
when he tripped over my body."*

—Rocky Graziano

Tennis was originally named "sphairistike," which in Greek means "to play."

•

Hall of Fame pitcher Sandy Koufax was born Sanford Braun.

•

The U.S. Lawn Tennis Championships are now known as the U.S. Open.

•

The Intercollegiate Conference of Faculty Representatives is better known as The Big Ten.

• • •

UNIFORMITY

The Portland Trail Blazers have retired the uniform numbers of Dave Twardzik (13) and Larry Steele (15). Their career scoring averages? 9.5 and 8.2 points per game, respectively.

•

The Indians retired the number 455 in honor of Cleveland's fans for their record number of consecutive sellouts at Jacobs Field from June of 1995 until April of 2001.

"The difference between golf and the government is that in golf you can't improve your lie."

—George Deukmejian, former California Governor

The Pittsburgh Pirates retired Honus Wagner's number 33- a number that he wore as a coach, but never as a player. They didn't wear uniform numbers in Wagner's playing days.

•

Mike Bratz wore number 23 before Michael Jordan arrived. Incidentally, Jordan donned three numbers in his NBA career- 23, 45, and 12. (He wore number 12 for a Bulls-Magic game after his jersey had been stolen.)

•

Lou Gehrig was the first baseball player to have his uniform number (4) retired.

•

When the Warriors traded Rick Barry to the Rockets in 1978, he found himself in a dilemma. He no longer could wear his No. 24, as it belonged to Houston's Moses Malone. Barry solved the problem by wearing the No. 2 at home games and the No. 4 on the road.

•

In honor of Wayne Gretzky, the number 99 will never again be worn in the NHL.

•

Pete Rose wore the same number on his back, 14 (for three different teams), for 24 years, the most in big league baseball history.

"There are three types of people…people who make things happen, people who watch things happen and people who don't know what's happening."
—John Madden

Mickey Mantle's home jersey #7 from 1960 sold for $101,410- about $40,000 more than his salary that year- at a sports memorabilia auction conducted by Lelands in Seaford, N.Y., in 2007.

•

Hank Aaron won the NL home run crown four times. Three of the four times, he finished the year with 44 homers - the number on his uniform. There's more on 44- When Al Downing gave up home run number 715 to Hank Aaron, Downing was also wearing that number.

•

The New York Knicks retired the number 613 in celebration of all the victories of coaching great Red Holzman.

•

Roberto Clemente wore 21 for most of his career with the Pittsburgh Pirates, but sported number 13 as a rookie.

•

The Dallas Cowboys were the first NFL team to display numbers on the sides of their pants.

•

In 1916, the Cleveland Indians became the first baseball players with numbers on their uniforms. The Tribe wore the numerals on their sleeves. The 1929 New York Yankees were the first team to

THOUGHTS OF THE THRONE

"He's a guy paid to talk while everyone goes to the bathroom."
—Sportscaster Bill Currie, explaining the
job of the color man on a broadcast

wear numbers on the back of their uniforms. Each player's number corresponded with his spot in the batting order.

• • •

THE ONE AND ONLY

Georgetown, located in the District of Columbia, is the only school to win the NCAA men's basketball championship that is not located in any of the fifty states. The Hoyas' lone title came in 1984, an 84-75 win over Houston.

•

Weeb Ewbank is the only coach to win titles in both the AFL and NFL. He won NFL titles in 1958 and 1959 with the Colts, and won the Super Bowl with the Jets in 1969.

•

Great Britain is the only country to participate in every Summer and Winter Olympics since the modern era Games began.

•

The only Hall of Famer to ever play for the Houston Colt .45s was Joe Morgan. (The Houston baseball franchise began play in 1962 and changed the team name to the Astros in '65.)

"Old age is when you resent the swimsuit issue of Sports Illustrated *because there are fewer articles to read."*

—George Burns

In 1919, horse racing legend Man O' War suffered his only defeat in 20 races, at the Sanford Memorial Stakes in Saratoga. The horse that beat him was appropriately named Upset.

•

In a 1920 game at the Polo Grounds, Ray Chapman suffered a fractured skull and died the next day as a result of being hit by a wild pitch from Yankee pitcher Carl Mays. The Indian shortstop is the only on-field player fatality in Major League Baseball history.

•

In 1968, Cardinals pitcher Ray Washburn no-hit the Giants at Candlestick Park, 2-0. The pitching gem came the day after Gaylord Perry of the Giants had no-hit St. Louis, 1-0. These games marked the only time that no-hitters have been thrown on successive days in the same ballpark.

•

Archie Griffin of Ohio State is the only two-time winner of the Heisman Trophy (1974 and '75).

•

Transsexual Renee Richards (nee Richard Raskind) is the only tennis player to compete in both the men's and women's singles at the U.S. Open.

"The way I putted, I must have been reading the greens in Spanish and putting them in English."

—Homero Blancas

Larry Brown is the only man to both play and coach for the United States basketball team in the Olympics. He was a player on the 1964 squad that beat the Soviet Union to win the gold in Tokyo. Then in Athens in 2004, Brown coached Team USA to their disappointing bronze medal, as Argentina claimed its first gold.

•

Roger Clemens is the only player to have been the MVP, the Cy Young Award winner and the All-Star Game MVP in the same year - all in 1986.

•

Carlos Baerga of the Cleveland Indians is the only player to hit a right-handed homer and a left-handed homer in the same inning. He did so in the seventh inning of a game against the New York Yankees on April 7, 1993.

•

Eddie Arcaro is the only jockey to win horse racing's Triple Crown twice.

•

Jim Thorpe is the only man to play in a World Series, win an Olympic gold medal, and be elected to the Pro Football Hall of Fame.

•

Rogers Hornsby is big league baseball's only .400/40 man. The for-

THOUGHTS OF THE THRONE

"Arnold Palmer is the biggest crowd pleaser since the invention of the portable sanitary facility."

—Bob Hope

mer Cardinal hit .401 and slugged 42 homers in 1922.

•

Brokers Tip won only one race in his career - the 1933 Kentucky Derby.

•

In 1971, Philadelphia's Rick Wise became the answer to a trivia question- the only pitcher to hit two home runs while recording a no-hitter. In addition to shutting down the Cincinnati Reds 4-0, Wise drove in three runs with his pair of homers.

•

Abbott and Costello are the only two members of the Baseball Hall of Fame not affiliated with baseball. The comedy team was honored for its zany *Who's on First?* routine.

•

In 1972, the Dallas Cowboys earned their first Super Bowl victory with a 24-3 win over the Miami Dolphins. In the loss, the Dolpins became the only team not to score a touchdown in the history of the game.

•

Rod Laver is the only man to win the tennis Grand Slam twice.

"Baseball is like a church. Many attend, but few understand."
—Wes Westrum

In 1997, University of Nebraska sophomore Jeremy Sonnenfeld became the only bowler in history to roll a perfect 900 series at an American Bowling Congress-sanctioned tournament in Omaha. Others had rolled three consecutive 300 games, but never in a single series.

• • •

THE LONG AND SHORT OF IT

5' 6" Hack Wilson is the shortest home run champion ever. He led the NL in homers in 1926, '27, '28 and '30. His 56 homers in 1930 stood as an NL record until 1998.

•

In 1951, Indianapolis and Rochester battled through six overtimes before Indianapolis prevailed, 75-73. Playing in the era before the 24-second shot clock, the teams held on to the ball as long as possible before shooting. It remains the longest game in NBA history.

•

Nolan Ryan had the longest career in baseball history, 27 years.

•

In 1969, the longest tennis match in Wimbledon history saw

"Absolute silence – that's one thing a sportswriter can quote accurately."
—Bobby Knight

Pancho Gonzales beat Charles Pasarell in a contest that lasted 5 hours and 12 minutes. The 41-year-old Gonzales won 22-24, 1-6, 16-14, 6-3 and 11-9 in the 112-game match.

•

In 1951, baseball's shortest player ever, 3' 7" Eddie Gaedel pinch-hit for the St. Louis Browns against the Detroit Tigers. Wearing the number "1/8," Gaedel - a brainchild of owner Bill Veeck - walked on four pitches. Veeck's p.r. stunt was not without precedent. In the '30s, Red Sox manager Joe Cronin sent a 3' 6" mascot to the plate in an exhibition game.

•

Until 1857, when baseball adopted the nine innings per game rule, the first team to score 21 runs was declared the winner.

•

At 5' 4", Ian Woosnam is the shortest winner of The Masters (1991).

•

The New York Giants needed only 51 minutes to defeat the Philadelphia Phillies, 6-1, September 28, 1919, in the major league's shortest nine-inning game in history.

•

The Sano Course at the Satsuki Golf Club in Japan lays claim to the world's longest golf hole- 964 yards.

> *"My neighbor is an avid golfer in the sense that if he had to choose between playing golf and achieving world peace, he'd want to know how many holes."*
> —Dave Barry, writer

Boston's Joe Oeschger and Brooklyn's Leon Cadore each went the distance in pitching their teams to a 1-1 tie in Major League Baseball's longest game- a 26 inning affair in 1920. The game was called on account of darkness.

•

Richard Sligh is the only seven-footer ever to play in the NFL, making eight appearances for the Oakland Raiders in 1967.

• • •

ALL IN THE FAMILY

On December 2, 2001, Bill and Martin Gramatica became the first brothers to win NFL games with overtime kicks on the same day. Bill kicked a 36-yard field goal 7:29 into overtime in the Cardinals 34-31 victory over the Raiders and Martin kicked a 21-yard FG 5:06 into OT in the Buccaneers 16-13 win against the Bengals.

•

Tony Gwynn Jr.'s first major league hit on July 19, 2006, came exactly 24 years to the day of his father's first big league hit — both doubles.

"I owe a lot to my parents, especially my mother and father."
—Greg Norman

In 1984, twins Phil and Steve Mahre finished first and second in the slalom at the Winter Olympics in Sarajevo, Yugoslavia. Phil turned in the better overall time to capture the gold.

•

Kiki Vandeweghe, a 14-year NBA veteran from 1980-93, is the son of former NBA player Ernie Vandeweghe and Colleen Kay Hutchins, who was Miss America in 1952. Kiki is also the nephew of another hoopster, four-time NBA All-Star Melvin Hutchins.

•

When his father Cecil played for Detroit, Prince Fielder would sometimes come along for batting practice and, even at the age of 12, was able to power the ball into the stands at Tiger Stadium.

•

WNBA star Cheryl Ford averaged a double-double as a rookie in 2003, leading the Detroit Shock to their first championship. Ford is the daughter of former NBA great Karl Malone, and like dad, played her college ball at Louisiana Tech.

•

Former WNBA and University of Connecticut basketball star Rebecca Lobo is married to *Sports Illustrated* writer Steve Rushin, who writes the weekly column "Air and Space" for the magazine.

> *When a pitcher's throwing a spit ball, don't worry*
> *and don't complain, just hit the dry side like I do."*
>
> —Stan Musial

Carl Lewis' 1984 Olympic gold medal for the 100 meters is buried with his father. At the 1987 funeral for his dad, Lewis put the medal in his father's hands, saying, "I want you to have this because it was your favorite event."

•

In 1979, brothers Joe and Phil Niekro led the National League in victories, each with 21.

•

Leon and Michael Spinks are the only two boxing brothers who won Olympic gold medals as amateurs and the heavyweight championship as professionals.

•

Pavel and Valeri Bure set the single season NHL goal-scoring record by brothers in the 1999-2000 season with 93 (58 by Pavel for Florida and 35 by Valeri for Calgary).

•

Father and son, Phil and Harold Johnson, were both KO'd by Jersey Joe Walcott- both in three rounds- both in Philadelphia, 14 years apart.

Max Baer Jr., who played Jethro Clampett on television's *Beverly Hillbillies*, is the son of the former heavyweight champion.

> *"All I'm asking for is what I want."*
> —Rickey Henderson

In 1973, hockey great Gordie Howe came out of retirement - but not to play in the NHL. Howe, who spent 26 years with the Detroit Red Wings, signed a million-dollar contract with the Houston Aeros of the World Hockey Association. Two of Howe's teammates on the Aeros were his sons, Mark and Marty.

•

The San Francisco Giants once had an outfield named "Alou." The three Alou brothers - Felipe, Jesus and Matty- played together in a game on September 15, 1963.

•

In 1936, Jesse Owens edged out fellow American Mack Robinson to capture the gold in the 200-meter dash at the Summer Olympics in Berlin. Few people remember Olympian Mack Robinson, but many recall his younger brother, baseball pioneer Jackie Robinson.

•

In 1990, Ken Griffey and Ken Griffey Jr., became the first father and son to play together on the same major league team, the Seattle Mariners. And it was "like father, like son," as they each singled in the first inning.

> *"Once when I was golfing in Georgia, I hooked the ball into the swamp. I went in after it and found an alligator wearing a shirt with a picture of a little golfer on it."*
> —Buddy Hackett

BABYFACE

At the 1998 Winter Games, 15-year-old Tara Lipinski became the youngest female Olympian to win the gold medal.

•

Jennifer Capriati was the youngest player to reach the finals of a major pro tennis tournament. The 13-year-old lost to Gabriela Sabatini, 6-4, 7-5, at the Virginia Slims of Florida, her first event after turning pro in 1990.

•

In 1986, Mike Tyson became the youngest man to win a heavyweight title. The 20-year-old boxer knocked out Trevor Berbick in the second round to capture the WBC crown.

•

As the head coach of the Super Bowl XLIII champion Pittsburgh Steelers, 36-year-old Mike Tomlin became the youngest ever to win a Super Bowl.

•

In 1985, 17-year-old Boris Becker became the youngest player to win at Wimbledon, beating Kevin Curren in four sets. Becker was also the first unseeded player to win the title.

"My ultimate dream is to have my own bank, maybe in Paris. I'd call it, 'Banks' Bank on the Left Bank.'"

—Ernie Banks

Freddy Adu is the youngest person ever to play in Major League Soccer history. He was 14 when he played his first game for D.C. United on April 3, 2004.

•

In 2001, at the age of 26, Karrie Webb became the youngest golfer in LPGA history to win the Grand Slam.

•

Dave DeBusschere, a player-coach for the Detroit Pistons at the age of 24, was the youngest coach in NBA history.

•

20-year-old Tony Conigliaro was the youngest player to win a home run crown when he led the AL in 1965 with 32 dingers.

•

Pitcher Joe Nuxhall made his debut with the Cincinnati Reds on June 10, 1944, at the age of 15 years, 10 months, and 11 days, becoming the youngest major leaguer ever.

•

At the age of 2, Tiger Woods putted against comedian Bob Hope on *The Mike Douglas Show* in 1978.

"If it wasn't for golf, I'd probably be a caddie today."
—George Archer

TRIVIA TIDBITS

In greyhound racing, if the dog catches the rabbit (because of mechanical failure), it's considered "no race."

•

Idi Amin, the former leader of Uganda, was the country's heavyweight boxing champ from 1951- 1960.

•

Nike is the Greek goddess of victory.

•

Eight months after winning four gold medals at the 1936 Olympics, Jesse Owens defeated Julio McCaw in the 100-yard dash- no big deal, except for the fact that McCaw was a race horse.

•

In earlier times, the Indianapolis 500 and other auto races had two people riding in the car: a driver and a mechanic.

•

In a boxing match in 1923, Canadian flyweight champion Gene LaRue and challenger Kid Pancho simultaneously KO'd each other with haymaker lefts. The referee counted both fighters out.

THOUGHTS OF THE THRONE

That's for the birds to eat. I'm afraid my players might start molting or going to the bathroom on newspapers."
—Manager Rocky Bridges, about nibbling on sunflower seeds

As a member of the New York Mets in 1963, Jimmy Piersall celebrated his 100th home run by running around the bases backwards.

•

Former standout wide receiver and current broadcaster Cris Collinsworth played on a winless Florida football team in college. The Gators were 0-11-1 in 1979.

•

In a 1963 basketball game in Alabama, West End High School defeated Glen Vocational, 97-54. Walter Garrett scored every single point for the winners.

•

Since NBA players cannot use their uniforms for advertising, Detroit Piston shooting guard Richard Hamilton decided to use his head. For several games in 2005, the Goodyear Tire and Rubber Company paid Hamilton to braid his hair in the style of the tread pattern of their Assurance TripleTred product.

•

There are 575 words in the epic poem *Casey at the Bat.*

•

Benjamin Franklin, Julius Caesar and Winston Churchill are all members of the International Swimming Hall of Fame in Ft. Lauderdale, Florida.

"We're fine. The only time we lose our concentration is when the umpire says, 'Play ball'."

—Lou Piniella, when asked if his team was mentally prepared

Jockey Eddie Arcaro's career got out of the gate slowly. Arcaro won 4,779 races - but rode 250 losers before his first victory.

•

The thoroughbred racing great, Affirmed, once got loose at Hollywood Park, prompting a trackwide search. The missing horse was located back in his own stall - which he had found among 2,244 others.

•

In the mid 1970's at Florida's Derby Lane greyhound track, one of the dogs was named Cilohocla. The origin of the dog's name remained a mystery until someone thought to reverse the spelling.

•

Heavyweight boxing champ Jack Dempsey bought a Rolls-Royce after each successful title fight - six in all.

•

The winner of the 1898 Boston Marathon was Ronald McDonald.

•

There are 1,661,220 inches in a marathon.

•

In 1957, jockey Willie Shoemaker misjudged the finish line at Churchill Downs, allowing Iron Liege to pass him and take the Kentucky Derby.

"I'm a firm believer that all sports will eventually be global. Someday, we may have a quarterback from China named Yao Fling."
—Paul Tagliabue, former NFL Commissioner

Former heavyweight champion Leon Spinks was once mugged. The thugs made off with his money and jewelry- in addition to his two gold front teeth.

•

It took 42 years and almost 10,000 games before the Harlem Globetrotters actually played in Harlem. Their first appearance "uptown" was in 1968.

•

Bad news/good news: Danny London, a popular deaf-mute boxer, lost a fight in 1929 after taking a ferocious punch to the head. The good news was, after he regained his senses, he found that he could hear and speak once again.

•

A couple of guys with the "right stuff" participated together in U.S. bombing missions over Korea. Co-piloting with Hall of Famer Ted Williams was astronaut John Glenn.

•

A.C. Gilbert was a United States pole-vaulter in the 1908 Olympics. A year later he was scaling new heights with his invention of the Erector Set.

•

Red Townley of Gadsen, Alabama, totalled the lowest bowling

> *"So far, the hardest part has been trying to come up with something that rhymes with Urlacher."*
>
> —Country music star Tim McGraw, on reworking the lyrics to his hit *I Like It, I Love It* to coincide with the *Monday Night Football* halftime highlight film

series ever containing a perfect game. His 1989 series included a pair of 88's followed by a 300 for a three-game total of 476.

•

Former Tennessee Titans running back Eddie George issued press credentials to his bachelor's party.

•

At age 19, rocker Rod Stewart abandoned a pro soccer career in Scotland to pursue musical opportunities.

•

Badminton began in India where it was originally called "poona."

•

The father of Mike Bacsik (who gave up Barry Bonds' 756th home run) was also a pitcher who, coincidentally, faced Henry Aaron when Hammerin' Hank had 755 homers.

•

Floyd Rood took 13 months to hit a golf ball across the United States. Rood began his golf ball-hitting journey in September 1963 at the Pacific Ocean. Thirteen months, 114,737 shots and 3,511 lost balls later, he arrived at the Atlantic.

•

Gerald Ford, a former All-Big Ten football center, received a toilet seat emblazoned with the University of Michigan seal. Ford liked

---

"I knew it was going to be a long season when, on Opening Day during the national anthem, one of my players turns to me and says, 'Every time I hear that song, I have a bad game.'"

—Manager Jim Leyland

the seat so much that he reportedly had it installed in the White House while he was President.

•

President Harry Truman had a bowling alley installed in the basement of the White House.

•

Only right-handed players can play polo according to the U.S. Polo Association. The governing body made the ruling in 1974 to cut down on collisions between lefties and righties.

• • •

LAST CALL

Lenny Wilkens is the last player-coach in NBA history.

•

Since Major League Baseball retired uniform number 42 in honor of Jackie Robinson, New York Yankees pitcher Mariano Rivera has the honor of being the last man to wear it.

Sandy Koufax won the most games for a pitcher in his final season, 27.

"We're not attempting to circumcise rules."
—Pittsburgh Steelers coach Bill Cowher

On January 14, 1968, Green Bay legend Vince Lombardi coached his last game with the Packers, a 33-14 win over the Oakland Raiders in Super Bowl II. Lombardi spent one more year on the sidelines, with the Washington Redskins, before dying of cancer in 1970.

•

Chicago Bears running back Gale Sayers was the last man to score six touchdowns in a single game, against the 49ers in 1965.

•

On the final pitch of his Hall of Fame career, Cardinals great Bob Gibson gave up a grand slam homer.

•

In 1971, Cleveland pitcher Steve Dunning hit a grand slam against Oakland. Unless the designated hitter rule is eliminated, Dunning is likely to go down in baseball history as the last AL pitcher to accomplish this feat.

•

In 1973, Chicago White Sox pitcher Wilbur Wood became the last hurler to start both games of a doubleheader. Wood didn't finish either contest and ended the day with a pair of losses to the Yankees.

"You must expect anything in golf. A stranger comes through, he's keen for a game, he seems affable enough, and on the eighth fairway he turns out to be an idiot."
—Alistair Cooke, writer

SPORTS - 20 QUESTIONS

1. Due to a scoring error discovered in 1999, what longtime baseball record was officially increased by 1, to 191?

2. As a sophomore at St.Vincent-St. Mary High School in Akron, Ohio, he was named First Team All State as a wide receiver. Indentify him.

3. What's the national sport of Canada?

4. How many feet long is a tennis court?

5. How many laps is the Indianapolis 500?

6. When catcher Jarrod Saltalamacchia was brought up to the majors in 2007, he immediately set what long-standing big league record?

7. True or false? The Los Angeles Angels first home was Wrigley Field.

8. Jackie Robinson's number 42 has been retired by Major League Baseball. In the NBA, one man is so honored by two teams with his #42 hanging in the rafters. The teams are Cleveland and Golden State. Who is he?

9. Name the former member of football's Raiders who played Apollo Creed in the *Rocky* flicks.

10. What's the maximum number of letters allowed in a race-horse's name?

11. Rollen Stewart (a.k.a. The Rainbow Man for his multi-colored wig) made it his mission to spread "the word" by displaying what sign which was often seen at stadium sporting events around the U.S.?

12. Who coined the term "Cablinasian?"

13. Duke defeated Oregon State, 20-16, in what major bowl game played in Durham, North Carolina, in 1942?

14. Name the people who portrayed Babe Ruth in *Pride of the Yankees*, Jackie Robinson in *The Jackie Robinson Story* and Muhammad Ali in *The Greatest*.

15. What former United States Senator's retired Knicks jersey could be seen overhead as he addressed the Democratic National Convention in Madison Square Garden?

16. Tom Seaver, Sparky Anderson and Babe Ruth all share the same first name. What is it?

17. True or false? The Olympic flame was conceived for the Games by none other than Adolf Hitler.

18. What was it in 1976 that *Sports Illustrated* called "the best halftime invention since the restroom?"

19. In 1940, Cleveland's Bob Feller hurled a 1-0 no-hitter against Chicago, yet none of the White Sox players' batting averages went up or down. How come?

20. Name the host city of the 2011 Super Bowl.

ANSWERS

1. Hack Wilson's RBI record, set in 1930.

2   LeBron James.

3. Lacrosse.

4. 78.

5. 200.

6. He became the player with MLB's longest surname.

7. True – It was an old Pacific Coast League park in Los Angeles owned by William Wrigley of bubble gum fame.

8. Nate Thurmond.

9. Carl Weathers.

10. 18.

11. JOHN 3:16.

12. Tiger Woods – He affably refers to his ethnic make-up by that name (a combination of Caucasian, Black, American-Indian, and Asian).

13. The Rose Bowl... Because it was less than a month after the Japanese attacked Pearl Harbor, it was decided to move the game to a less vulnerable site.

14. They all played themselves.

15. Bill Bradley's number 24.

16. George.

17 True.

18. The first NBA Slam Dunk Contest.

19. It was Opening Day.

20. Dallas.